P9-BJO-550

BIOMES

OF THE WORLD

VOLUME 6

Temperate Forests

Michael Allaby

GROLIER
EDUCATIONAL

About This Set

BIOMES OF THE WORLD is a nine-volume set that describes all the major landscapes (biomes) that are found across the Earth. Biomes are large areas of the world where living conditions for plants and animals are broadly similar, so that the vegetation in these locations appears much the same. Each of the books in this set describes one or more of the main biomes: Volume 1: The Polar Regions (tundra, ice cap, and permanent ice); Volume 2: Deserts (desert and semidesert); Volume 3: Oceans (oceans and islands); Volume 4: Wetlands (lakes, rivers, marshes, and estuaries); Volume 5: Mountains (mountain and highland); **Volume 6: Temperate Forests** (boreal coniferous forest or taiga, coastal coniferous forest, broad-leaf and mixed forest, Mediterranean forest and scrub); Volume 7: Tropical Forests (rain forest and monsoon forest); Volume 8: Temperate Grasslands (prairie, steppe, and pampas); Volume 9: Tropical Grasslands (savanna).

The books each have three sections. The first describes the geographical location of the biome, its climate, and other physical features that make it the way it is. The second section describes the plants and animals that inhabit the biome and the ways in which they react to each other. The final section of each book deals with the threats to the biome and what is being done to reduce these. An introduction in Volume 1 includes a map showing all the biomes described in this set, and a map showing all the countries of the world.

Throughout the pages of this set there are diagrams explaining the processes described in the text, artwork depictions of animals and plants, diagrams showing ecosystems, and tables. The many color photographs bring each biome to life. At the end of each book there is a glossary explaining the meaning of technical words used, a list of other sources of reference (books and websites), followed by an index to all the volumes in the set.

**Published 1999 by Grolier Educational,
Danbury, CT 06816**

*This edition published exclusively for the school
and library market*

**Planned and produced by
Andromeda Oxford Limited,
11–13 The Vineyard, Abingdon, Oxon
OX14 3PX, UK**

Copyright © Andromeda Oxford Limited 1999

All rights reserved. No part of this publication may be reproduced, stored in a retrieval system, or transmitted in any form or by any means electronic, mechanical, photocopying, recording, or otherwise, without the permission of the copyright holder.

Project Manager: *Graham Bateman*
Editors: *Jo Newson, Penelope Isaac*
Art Editor and Designer: *Steve McCurdy*
Cartography: *Richard Watts, Tim Williams*
Editorial Assistant: *Marian Dreier*
Picture Manager: *Claire Turner*
Production: *Nicolette Colborne*

Origination by Expo Holdings Sdn Bhd, Malaysia
Printed in Hong Kong

Set ISBN 0-7172-9341-6
Volume 6 ISBN 0-7172-9347-5

Biomes of the world.
        p.   cm.
    Includes indexes.
    Contents: v. 1. Polar regions -- v. 2. Deserts -- v. 3. Oceans -- v. 4. Wetlands -- v. 5. Mountains -- v. 6. Temperate forests -- v. 7. Tropical forests -- v. 8. Temperate grassland -- v. 9. Tropical grassland.
    Summary: In nine volumes, explores each of the earth's major ecological regions, defining important features, animals, and environmental issues.
    ISBN 0-7172-9341-6 (hardcover : set : alk. paper). -- ISBN 0-7172-9347-5 (hardcover : vol. 6 : alk. paper)
    1. Biotic communities--juvenile literature. 2. Life zones--Juvenile literature. 3. Ecology--Juvenile literature. [1. Biotic communities.] I. Grolier Educational (Firm)
QH541.14.B57   1999
577--dc21   98-37524
                                                  CIP
                                                  AC

Contents

The Physical World of Temperate Forests

*W*arm summers, fairly short winters, and rainfall every month of the year combine to produce the beautiful deciduous forests, whose trees have leaves that change color with the seasons. In the harsher climates to the north deciduous forests are replaced by evergreen forests that stretch across northern Canada, Europe, and Asia. In the drier areas to the south evergreen shrubs that are prone to catch fire dominate.

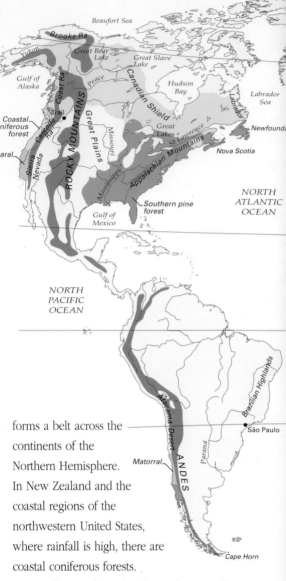

Temperate forests—made up of three different biomes—occur in the temperate regions of the world. The temperate regions lie in two broad bands across the Northern and Southern Hemispheres. In the North the temperate regions occur between the Tropic of Cancer at latitude 23°30' N and the Arctic Circle at 66°30' N; in the south the temperate regions lie between the Tropic of Capricorn at latitude 23°30' S, and the Antarctic Circle at 66°30' S.

Nearly three-quarters of all temperate forests are in North America and the countries of the former Soviet Union, principally the Russian Federation. North America has 1,764,000 square miles (4,568,760 sq. km) of forest and Russia an astounding 3,151,000 square miles (8,161,090 sq. km). Most of this is the boreal coniferous (evergreen, cone-bearing) forest (or taiga), which

forms a belt across the continents of the Northern Hemisphere. In New Zealand and the coastal regions of the northwestern United States, where rainfall is high, there are coastal coniferous forests.

Farther south as the climate becomes less severe conifers give way to mostly deciduous trees (trees that shed their leaves at the end of each growing season). These form the major part of the temperate broad-leaved forest biome and are typical of large areas of the northeastern United States and western Europe. Close relatives of the pines of the boreal forests also grow in many parts of the United States (such as the southern pine forests), wherever the climate is too dry for deciduous trees. Also included in this

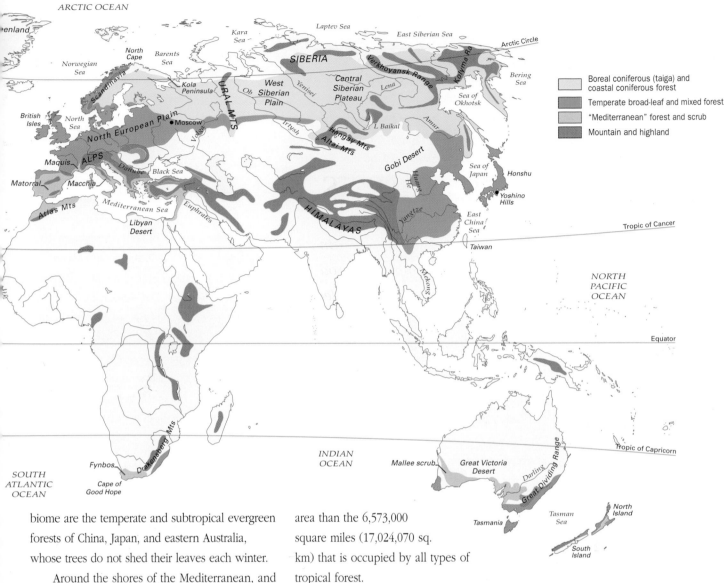

ARCTIC OCEAN

Laptev Sea

East Siberian Sea

Arctic Circle

enland

Kara Sea

Norwegian Sea

North Cape

Barents Sea

SIBERIA

Verkhoyansk Range

Kolyma Ra

Bering Sea

Kola Peninsula

URAL MTS

West Siberian Plain

Central Siberian Plateau

Yenisei

Lena

Sea of Okhotsk

Scandinavia

British Isles

North Sea

North European Plain

•Moscow

Volga

Ob

Irtysh

Hangay Mts

Altai Mts

L Baikal

Amur

Sea of Japan

Honshu

Maquis

ALPS

Danube

Black Sea

Gobi Desert

Hu

Yoshino Hills

Matorral

Macchia

Huang

Atlas Mts

Mediterranean Sea

Euphrates

HIMALAYAS

Yangtze

East China Sea

Libyan Desert

Tropic of Cancer

Taiwan

NORTH PACIFIC OCEAN

Mekong

Equator

Tropic of Capricorn

Drakensberg Mts

INDIAN OCEAN

Mallee scrub

Great Victoria Desert

Darling

Great Dividing Range

SOUTH ATLANTIC OCEAN

Fynbos

Cape of Good Hope

Tasman Sea

North Island

Tasmania

South Island

	Boreal coniferous (taiga) and coastal coniferous forest
	Temperate broad-leaf and mixed forest
	"Mediterranean" forest and scrub
	Mountain and highland

biome are the temperate and subtropical evergreen forests of China, Japan, and eastern Australia, whose trees do not shed their leaves each winter.

Around the shores of the Mediterranean, and in Australia, parts of South Africa, in Chile, and in California there are other forests that are made up of broad-leaved evergreen trees. These make up the "Mediterranean" forest and scrub biome that is known as chapparal in California and elsewhere by other local names, such as maquis in France, matorral in Spain and Chile, and mallee scrub in Australia.

Together the temperate forests cover a total area of approximately 6,643,000 square miles (17,205,370 sq. km), which is a slightly greater area than the 6,573,000 square miles (17,024,070 sq. km) that is occupied by all types of tropical forest.

Not all of the land in the temperate regions is forested, of course. Above a certain height, which varies according to latitude, trees do not grow on mountains, so there are no forests on high mountain ranges such as the Rocky Mountains, Andes, Alps, and Himalayas. In the interior of continents, far from the nearest ocean, the climate is usually too dry for trees to grow. Some of these areas support grassland, others are desert. In the far north, too, the climate is too dry and too cold for trees to grow. This is the

TEMPERATE FOREST is found over most of Europe and the east and west of North America. Boreal coniferous forest forms a broad belt across Canada, northern Europe, and Asia. In the Southern Hemisphere less land extends into temperate regions, so there is less temperate forest there.

THE GLOBAL WIND SYSTEM *(below).* **Winds are driven by the circulation of the atmosphere. Warm air rises at the equator, descends in the tropics, and some of it flows back toward the equator as the trade winds. The trade winds of both hemispheres meet in the intertropical convergence zone (ITCZ). Cold air sinks over the North and South Poles and flows outward into lower latitudes, then rises as it meets tropical air flowing toward the poles.**

region supporting tundra vegetation such as sedges, mosses, grasses, and lichens. Tundra—a treeless region with permanently frozen subsoil—extends over the low-lying part of northern Canada, around the coast of Alaska, and over the western and southern coasts of Greenland. It also occurs across northern Europe and Asia, from the Kola Peninsula on the north side of the White Sea eastward all the way to the Pacific Ocean.

Temperate forests are much more extensive in the Northern Hemisphere than the Southern, and there is no belt of coniferous forest in the Southern Hemisphere. This is because there is much less land in the Southern than in the Northern Hemisphere, and most of it lies in the tropics. Only the part of South America south of São Paulo, the tip of southern Africa and Madagascar, about half of Australia, and all of

New Zealand lie in the temperate region of the Southern Hemisphere. Cape Horn is the most southerly point, at 55°59' S, almost exactly the latitude of Moscow in the Northern Hemisphere.

TEMPERATE FOREST AND TEMPERATE CLIMATE

In the middle latitudes of both hemispheres the prevailing—or usual—winds blow from west to east. That is also the direction in which weather systems usually travel. The western coasts of the continents receive winds and weather that have crossed the ocean, the eastern coasts winds and weather that have traveled over land. In the Arctic and Antarctic regions on one side of the middle latitudes, and in the tropics on the other, the winds are mainly from the east.

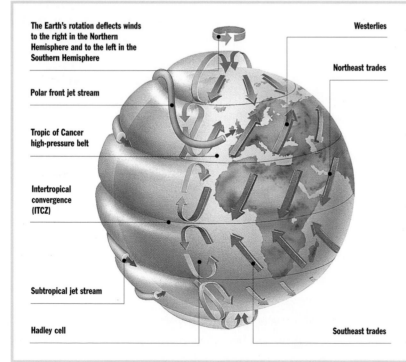

The Earth's rotation deflects winds to the right in the Northern Hemisphere and to the left in the Southern Hemisphere

Polar front jet stream

Tropic of Cancer high-pressure belt

Intertropical convergence (ITCZ)

Subtropical jet stream

Hadley cell

Westerlies

Northeast trades

Southeast trades

Rossby waves develop in the polar front, often over a cycle lasting several weeks. They affect the polar front jet stream, which lies close to the polar front. Mountain ranges affect the flow of air, triggering the formation of very long waves in the polar front, where cold, arctic air meets warm, tropical air

The waves become steeper, carrying cold air far to the south and warm air far to the north

Finally, the polar front and its jet stream break into separate cells. The jet stream blows around the cells, which are of warm and cold air. These remain stationary, sometimes for weeks, while weather systems move around them, so they bring prolonged spells of clear or wet weather

This distribution of winds results from the fact that the Sun heats the Earth more strongly at the equator than it does at the poles. At the equator air is warmed strongly by contact with the surface of the land and ocean. When air is warmed, it expands because its molecules have more energy to move away from each other, and when air expands, a given volume of it contains fewer molecules, so it becomes less dense. Since the air is less dense than air above it, it rises like a bubble. As it rises, it also cools because its molecules expend the energy they gained when they were warmed, and it moves away from the equator, pushed by air rising behind it.

High over the tropics the cold equatorial air meets air warmer and less dense than itself and sinks beneath it all the way to the surface. There, some of the air flows back toward the equator, and the rest flows in the opposite direction.

Over the polar regions very cold, dense air is sinking to the surface and flowing outward. In middle latitudes the polar air moving away from

CONIFEROUS FORESTS, such as this one in Russia, cover a broad band of land across northern Canada, Europe, and Asia. This belt of northern forest is known as the taiga.

FALL COLORS in the trees growing on the sides of a canyon in western New York State. The canyon has been carved over many centuries by the Genesee River. The presence of broad-leaved deciduous trees indicates that the ground does not dry out in summer or remain frozen for long in winter.

the pole meets tropical air moving toward the pole, and air rises.

The Coriolis Effect

The Earth is spinning on its own axis, completing one revolution every 24 hours. Because the Earth is a sphere, during that 24 hours a point on the equator must travel a greater distance than a point at a higher latitude. To do that the two points must travel at different speeds. Quito, Ecuador, which lies almost on the equator, is moving eastward at about 1,037 mph

(1,668 km/h), and New York is moving at about 794 mph (1,277 km/h).

Air is moving eastward at the same speed as the land or ocean surface beneath it. If it moves toward or away from the equator, it will retain that motion. Equatorial air, for example, is still traveling eastward at more than 1,000 mph (1,609 km/h) as it moves out of the tropics. The surface beneath it is moving more slowly, however. If equatorial air moved all the way to the latitude of New York, it would be moving eastward about 243 mph (391 km/h) faster than the land or sea surface (1,037−794=243). Seen from the surface, the air would appear to be deflected to the east.

This effect was discovered in 1835 by the French physicist Gaspard de Coriolis and is known as the Coriolis effect. It causes moving air —as well as ocean currents and any traveling object not attached to the surface, including aircraft—to be deflected to the right in the Northern Hemisphere and to the left in the Southern Hemisphere. The size of the effect is proportional to the speed of the moving air and the latitude.

The Coriolis effect is strongest at the poles and zero at the equator. It means that instead of air rushing in and filling areas where air pressure is low, or rushing out of areas where pressure is high, the moving air flows around these areas. North of the equator it flows counterclockwise around areas of low pressure and clockwise around areas of high pressure. Without the Coriolis effect air pressure would be the same everywhere, and world climates would be very different. The middle latitudes would almost certainly be too dry for trees, and there would be no temperate forests.

Fronts and Jet Streams

The boundaries between polar and tropical air and between tropical and midlatitude air are called "fronts"—the polar front and subtropical front respectively. At the top of each of these fronts, at altitudes of 30,000–50,000 feet (9,144–15,240 m), the sharp temperature difference between the air on either side produces a very strong wind called a jet stream. In winter, when the temperature difference is

strongest, the polar front jet stream sometimes blows at 300 mph (483 km/h).

The jet streams blow with the cold air on their left in the Northern Hemisphere and with the cold air on their right in the Southern Hemisphere, which means they blow from west to east in both hemispheres. The polar front jet stream does not blow all the time or always at the same speed.

Every so often, over a cycle usually lasting three to eight weeks, waves develop along the polar front jet stream. These are known as Rossby waves (they were discovered in 1940 by the Swedish-American meteorologist Carl-Gustav Rossby). The waves grow bigger, and eventually pockets of warm or cold air that have formed in the loops become detached, so the jet stream breaks into a series of circles. Depressions—areas

TREE RHODODENDRONS FORM FORESTS in the lower Himalayas, growing beside junipers and magnolias. At higher elevations there are more shrublike species of rhododendrons, which give way to meadows as the climate becomes too cold and dry for woody plants.

of low surface atmospheric pressure that produce wet weather—form beneath the jet stream and are dragged along by it. This is why weather systems usually move from west to east in middle latitudes, but can travel to the north or south below Rossby waves. When the jet stream breaks down, areas of high and low pressure remain stationary, bringing spells of clear or wet weather that can last for a week or two.

WEATHER AND TEMPERATE FORESTS

Air in the middle latitudes moves beneath the polar front jet stream. As it crosses the oceans, water evaporates into it, making it moist and bringing rain or snow to the forests of the temperate regions. In these areas rain and snow fall in every month of the year. Plants can absorb only liquid water, though (ice is useless to them because they cannot take it up through their roots), so a cold winter and frozen ground bring drought to plants, even if there is a deep layer of snow.

Plants survive the winter drought in different ways. Deciduous trees such as oaks, maples, and beeches shed their leaves and become dormant (they are still alive but not growing). Coniferous trees such as spruces, firs, and pines keep their leaves, but they do not allow more than the very minimum amount of water to be lost through them. This strategy works best where the drought is prolonged. Coniferous forests flourish in the far north, where winters are hard and long. Deciduous forests grow in areas where winters are shorter.

A SOIL PROFILE is a section cut vertically through a soil, from ground level to the underlying bedrock. A well-developed soil reveals horizontal layers, called horizons. These are identified by capital letters followed by numbers for subdivisions of each horizon and sometimes by additional letters indicating the chemical composition.

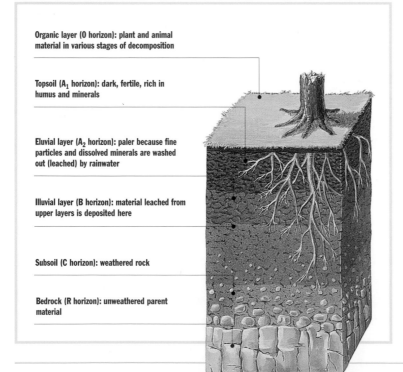

Organic layer (O horizon): plant and animal material in various stages of decomposition

Topsoil (A_1 horizon): dark, fertile, rich in humus and minerals

Eluvial layer (A_2 horizon): paler because fine particles and dissolved minerals are washed out (leached) by rainwater

Illuvial layer (B horizon): material leached from upper layers is deposited here

Subsoil (C horizon): weathered rock

Bedrock (R horizon): unweathered parent material

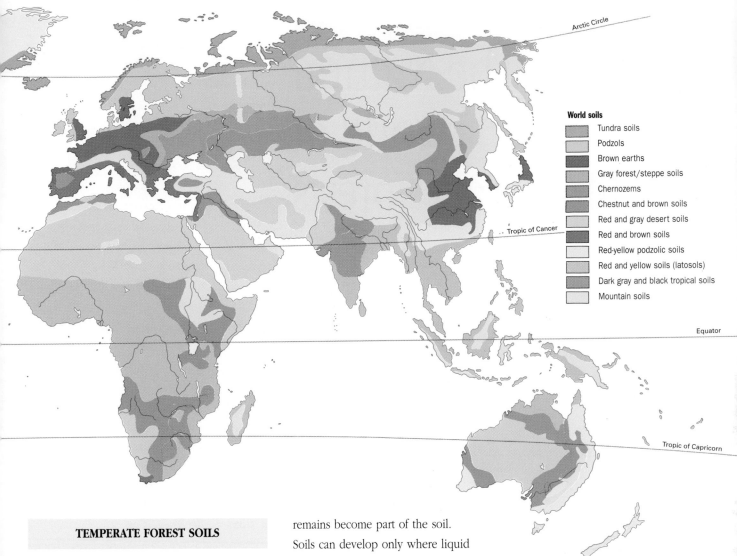

World soils

- Tundra soils
- Podzols
- Brown earths
- Gray forest/steppe soils
- Chernozems
- Chestnut and brown soils
- Red and gray desert soils
- Red and brown soils
- Red-yellow podzolic soils
- Red and yellow soils (latosols)
- Dark gray and black tropical soils
- Mountain soils

Arctic Circle

Tropic of Cancer

Equator

Tropic of Capricorn

TEMPERATE FOREST SOILS

Soils consist of tiny particles that have been broken or scoured away from the underlying rock. Water moving around and between the particles causes chemical reactions that release chemical compounds; plants use these to build and maintain their own tissues.

Plants start growing as soon as there are enough of these plant nutrients to sustain them. Plant roots make channels through the soil, and dead plant material becomes mixed with the small particles. Animals arrive to feed on the plants, and on each other, and their wastes and remains become part of the soil. Soils can develop only where liquid water is present: in deserts and the permanently frozen lands around the poles soil development is extremely slow.

Temperate climates bring ample water. In temperate regions the soils are often deep and rich in nutrients. Trees, with their large root systems, grow well here. Once established, forests contribute to the development of their soils. Dead leaves or needles, fallen branches and whole trees, and roots that die below ground are food for the vast community of animals, fungi, and microorganisms that recycles the nutrients, maintaining the fertility of the soil.

SOILS OF THE WORLD vary according to the rock from which they have developed and the climates in which they have formed.

The Natural World of Temperate Forests

*I*n the deep shade of the forest floor all is still. The air is calm, and the forest is silent except for the distant call of birds and the occasional rustling of some small animal busily making its way through the carpet of dry leaves. It feels as though the forest has stood, just as it is now, for countless millions of years, and that it will continue to stand as it is until the end of time. Yet it is changing constantly. It has not always existed, and one day it may disappear for entirely natural reasons.

About 18,000 years ago the last ice age was at its most extreme. In North America a thick sheet of ice extended to about where Indianapolis is today. Most of Europe also lay beneath the ice.

There was no soil in the ice-covered areas. Soil that existed before the spread of the ice sheets had been scoured away because ice is constantly moving, dragging loose rocks and soil with it. Beyond the edge of the ice there was tundra, like the tundra that exists today in northern Canada and Siberia, and beyond the tundra there were forests.

Then the climate changed and temperatures rose. About 10,000 years ago the ice started to melt at the edges. As the ice retreated north, bare rock was exposed, much of it pulverized into gravel or sand by the weight of ice. The ice itself melted into water. Rivers of meltwater flowed across the land. It was not a steady retreat. Several times conditions turned colder, and the ice started advancing again, but each advance led to a retreat that left the edge of the ice a little farther to the north.

Moss and lichen spores (reproductive bodies that can become new individuals), carried many miles on the air, drifted to the ground. Here and there these spores found conditions they could tolerate. Then seeds, blown by the wind or dropped by birds, began to germinate (sprout). Sedges and rushes grew in wet places, grasses and flowering herbs on the drier ground, in sheltered places. Soil began accumulating in

THE SPREAD OF FOREST AFTER THE ICE. As the last ice age ended, plants began to grow on land that had been covered by ice. Soil developed, more plants arrived, and in time trees began to appear. As they spread and multiplied, vast areas came to be forested.

As the ice retreated, plants moved north, following the edge of the ice. First lichens and mosses arrived, then flowering plants, and eventually coniferous trees such as junipers and pines and hardy broad-leaved trees such as birches

The junipers, pines, and birches continued expanding northward. In the south they were replaced by broad-leaved trees such as oaks, elms, limes, and alders. These formed deciduous forest south of the coniferous forest

The forests continued to change, adapting all the time to changes in the climate. People contributed to the change by clearing areas to provide land for farming and pasture. Today most of the original broad-leaved forest has gone, but the coniferous forest to the north has been little altered by humans

creviccs between rocks. As the layer of soil became thicker, bigger plants were able to establish themselves in it. The tundra vegetation, always growing near the edge of the ice, followed the retreating ice sheets.

Tundra plants can grow in shallow soil, most of them low to the ground as protection against the bitter wind that dries their leaves, but they cannot tolerate being in the shade. As the climate continued to grow warmer, other plants were able to survive in the north. Trees started to arrive. Birches (*Betula* species) and junipers (*Juniperus* species) were the first. Dwarf birch (*B. nana*) grows to a height of no more than 3 feet (1 m) and still flourishes on the edge of the tundra and on mountainsides. Common juniper (*J. communis*) is often a low shrub, although under favorable conditions it can grow into a small tree.

Pine trees (*Pinus* species) began to appear. They shaded the birch seedlings, restricting their growth, and birch became less common. Spruces (*Picea* species) joined the pines. They tolerate cold, wet soils, and provided there is sufficient depth of soil to anchor them, they will also withstand strong winds.

As more tree species continued to arrive, shading out the tundra plants, the edge of the coniferous forest moved steadily northward. If, in years to come, the climate grows warmer, the coniferous forest will spread still farther into the north.

By about 9,000 years

CHANGING HABITATS.
Plants and animals alter their surroundings in ways that allow other species to establish themselves. Gradually, in a process known as "succession," one plant and animal community replaces another until a stable "climax" community is formed.

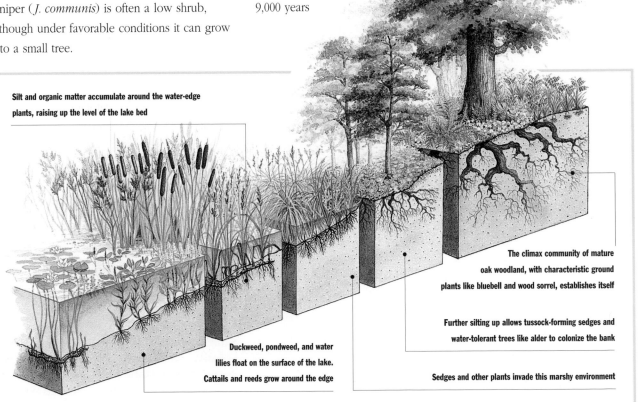

Silt and organic matter accumulate around the water-edge plants, raising up the level of the lake bed

The climax community of mature oak woodland, with characteristic ground plants like bluebell and wood sorrel, establishes itself

Further silting up allows tussock-forming sedges and water-tolerant trees like alder to colonize the bank

Duckweed, pondweed, and water lilies float on the surface of the lake. Cattails and reeds grow around the edge

Sedges and other plants invade this marshy environment

ago the coniferous forest was giving way along its southern edge to trees better suited to warmer, wetter weather. The forests of broad-leaved trees were also expanding northward. In Europe hazel (*Corylus* species) was followed by elm (*Ulmus* species), oak (*Quercus* species), and alder (*Alnus* species). In eastern North America spruce and fir (*Abies* species) forest was giving way to pine and oak, and around 7,000 years ago this was changing to forests of oak, beech (*Fagus* species), and a coniferous species, hemlock (genus *Tsuga*).

Climates continued to change, now becoming warmer, now cooler, now wetter, now drier, and with each change the composition of the forests changed. The forests that developed naturally would not have remained unaltered even if European and Native American farmers had not begun the process of changing them.

HOW COMMUNITIES ARE ESTABLISHED

Starting with bare ground or a pool of water in which nothing lives, plants and the animals that feed on them arrive as groups. First there are the opportunists, plants that produce huge numbers of small, wind-borne seeds that germinate quickly. These plants blanket the ground, but as later arrivals grow up around them, they are shaded or starved of nutrient by the roots of the new arrivals. The opportunists disappear and so, in time, do the small plants that displaced them.

Over a long period the changes can be dramatic. As more plants grow around the edges of a lake, for example, their remains accumulate on the bottom, and water absorbed from the lake by their roots evaporates from their leaves. The lake becomes shallower, so the plants can advance farther and farther into it. Finally, the plants transform what was a lake into wet ground, then dry out the ground. Most ponds and small lakes eventually disappear in this way.

This chain of events, leading from bare land or water through a number of distinct communities of plants and animals, is called succession. Eventually, the community reaches a stable condition, after which change happens more slowly. This semipermanent community is called a climax. Temperate forest is the natural climax over most of lowland Europe and many parts of North America.

LOSS OF ENERGY THROUGH THE FOOD CHAIN *(below)*. The amount of energy transferred between organisms in a food chain is only 10–15 percent. Up to 85 percent of energy is wasted at each level, most of it lost as heat when organisms respire. An animal at the top of the chain—often a predator—receives only a fraction of the original energy available.

NATURAL FOREST in the Bavarian Forest National Park, in southern Germany *(right)*. **This has been allowed to develop without human interference. Fallen trees are not removed, trees are not felled, and plants are allowed to grow wherever they can.**

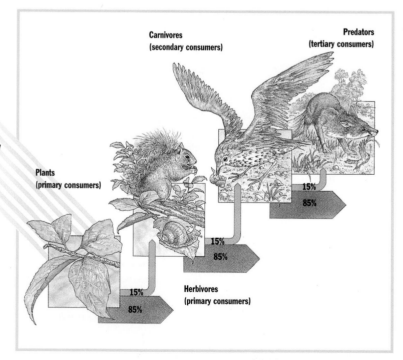

Solar energy

Carnivores (secondary consumers)

Predators (tertiary consumers)

Plants (primary consumers)

Herbivores (primary consumers)

15%
85%

15%
85%

15%
85%

15%
85%

MATURE BEECH TREES cast a deep shade over the floor of this forest, discouraging the growth of smaller trees and shrubs. Mammals of the forest live mainly on the floor because the shedding of leaves each fall alters the environment in the forest canopy, making it impossible for a stable community to assemble.

FOOD AND ENERGY

Herbivorous (plant-eating) animals feed on plants, carnivorous (meat-eating) animals feed on herbivores (and usually eat some plants as well), and the wastes from all of these—leaves, fallen branches, dead plants and animals—are decomposed to release chemical compounds that are absorbed by plant roots, enabling the plants to grow. Everything depends on everything else through a very complex network of relationships.

The study of these relationships is called ecology, and a community studied in this way is called an ecosystem.

Green plants are the base of the entire system, because it is only green plants that can capture the energy of sunlight and use it to manufacture sugars in the process called photosynthesis. When an animal eats a plant, it absorbs in its food a share of the energy captured by the plant. When a carnivore eats a herbivore, it takes its share of that energy. Plants do not capture sunlight or animals eat plants simply to pass on energy to animals that eat them, however. They use the energy themselves to build and maintain their own bodies, releasing it by the process of respiration. Respiration produces heat, most of which is released into the surroundings and lost. Every plant and every animal uses at least 85 percent of the energy it obtains for its own purposes. This leaves no more than 15 percent—and usually less—to be passed on. In the end all the energy captured by green plants is turned into heat.

This limits the number of times energy can be exchanged. A mouse, for example, can find all the food it needs in quite a small area. But for an owl to obtain the amount of energy it needs, it must eat many mice, so the owl needs a much larger area in which to hunt. An animal trying to hunt owls would need an even bigger area to capture enough of them for its needs. A point is soon reached beyond which more energy is required to find the food than can be obtained through eating it. That is why large carnivorous animals are always few and far between.

HOW A TREE WORKS

Below ground tree roots run in every direction, filling the forest soil. The arrangement varies between species, but the roots of many full-grown trees spread 50 to 80 feet (15 to 24 m) from the base of the trunk—farther than the branches. Most coniferous trees have shallow roots that spread to the sides, but broad-leaved trees usually have a taproot—a root that grows straight downward, often all the way to the level below which the ground is saturated with water.

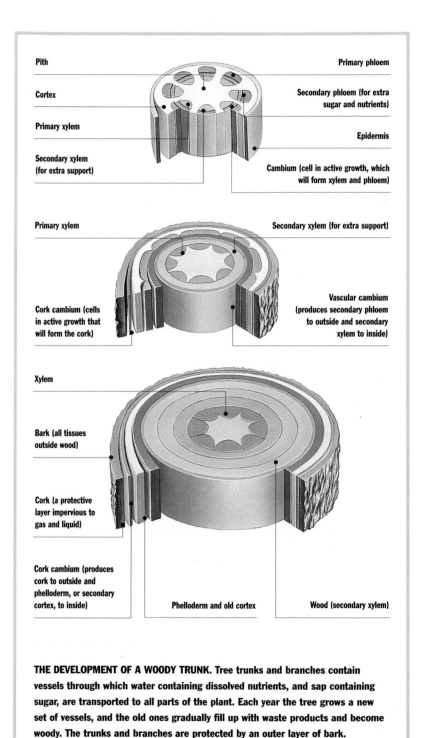

Pith

Cortex

Primary xylem

Secondary xylem
(for extra support)

Primary phloem

Secondary phloem (for extra
sugar and nutrients)

Epidermis

Cambium (cell in active growth, which
will form xylem and phloem)

Primary xylem

Cork cambium (cells
in active growth that
will form the cork)

Secondary xylem (for extra support)

Vascular cambium
(produces secondary phloem
to outside and secondary
xylem to inside)

Xylem

Bark (all tissues
outside wood)

Cork (a protective
layer impervious to
gas and liquid)

Cork cambium (produces
cork to outside and
phelloderm, or secondary
cortex, to inside)

Phelloderm and old cortex

Wood (secondary xylem)

THE DEVELOPMENT OF A WOODY TRUNK. Tree trunks and branches contain vessels through which water containing dissolved nutrients, and sap containing sugar, are transported to all parts of the plant. Each year the tree grows a new set of vessels, and the old ones gradually fill up with waste products and become woody. The trunks and branches are protected by an outer layer of bark.

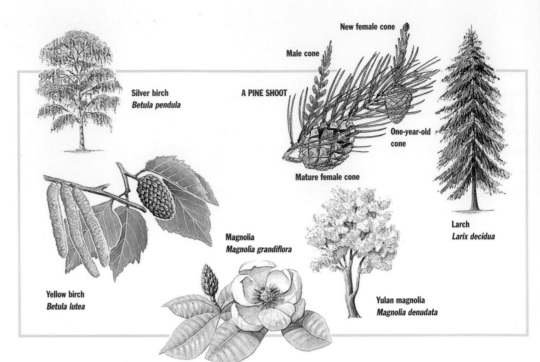

Silver birch
Betula pendula

A PINE SHOOT

Male cone

New female cone

One-year-old cone

Mature female cone

Larch
Larix decidua

Yellow birch
Betula lutea

Magnolia
Magnolia grandiflora

Yulan magnolia
Magnolia denudata

GYMNOSPERMS AND ANGIOSPERMS differ in the way they produce seeds. Most gymnosperms are conifers. Male cones, such as those of the pine (*Pinus* species), release pollen that is carried on the wind to the female cones *(center right)*. Many coniferous trees have a characteristic shape, such as that of the larch *(Larix decidua)*. Angiosperms produce flowers. Birch trees (*Betula* species) are wind pollinated; magnolias are pollinated by insects. Most angiosperm trees are quite different in shape from gymnosperms. Silver birch *(B. pendula)* and Yulan magnolia *(M. denudata)* are typical angiosperms (see page 20).

Roots anchor the tree. They also absorb water and the nutrients dissolved in it. Roots have branches, ending in masses of very fine hairs. Liquid can pass through the walls of these root hairs and into the plant. There the liquid enters elongated cells joined end to end and with holes in the walls separating each cell from its neighbor. These cells, called vessel elements, form tissue called xylem; eventually the xylem reaches every smallest twig and leaf, bringing water and nutrients.

In the leaves cells manufacture sugars out of water and carbon dioxide, using the energy of sunlight to drive the chemical reactions. The sugars dissolve in water, and this solution enters another system of elongated cells that make up tissue called phloem or bast, through which it is transported to all the living cells of the plant.

Wood and Bark

Each year a growing tree produces new phloem and xylem tissue, and old cells die. In spring the tree grows new xylem cells that are large and have thin walls. Xylem cells that grow in summer are smaller and have thicker walls. In late summer cell production ceases. The two types of cell produce two rings, one light in color and the other dark. These annual growth rings, or tree rings, can be used to count the age of the tree.

The walls of vessel elements contain lignin, a tough substance that strengthens the cells. As they grow older, these cells gradually lose the ability to transport liquids, and they fill with waste products excreted from the living cells around them. The wastes include more lignin, and the vessel elements change into wood.

A tree trunk or branch consists of several distinct layers of tissue. On the outside there is a layer of cork. This is dead tissue containing a waxy substance called suberin: it protects the living tissue from damage, the entry or loss of water, and cold. Cork is constantly being shed from the outside of the tree. The phloem lies immediately beneath the cork. As phloem cells die, they form part of the cork, and together the cork and phloem layers make up the bark. If a cut is made all the way around the tree through the bark, sugars from the leaves will no longer be able to reach the roots, and the tree will die. Cutting a tree in this way is called ring barking.

TAIGA, THE FOREST OF THE NORTH

In Greek mythology Boreas was the god of the north wind. His name gives us the adjective "boreal," meaning northern. The boreal forest, or forest of the north, forms a broad belt south of the tundra that is also known as the taiga.

The taiga extends across southern Alaska and Canada, and in Eurasia from northern Norway and Sweden all the way to the Pacific Ocean, including eastern China and northern Japan. Winters are cold and summers short in the lands of the taiga. July is usually the warmest month. Then the temperature can reach 60°F (15°C), although it is usually lower. In January, usually the coldest month, the average temperature is about 5°F (–15°C) in some places but –40°F (–40°C) in others.

Precipitation is low, ranging from 1.6 to 4 inches (40 to 100 mm) a year, but the winter snowfall is heavy, and little water evaporates because of the low temperature, so the ground is wet. There are many ponds, lakes, bogs, and "muskegs," areas of wet peat with trees and shrubs growing on them.

The trees that grow in this region are conifers; although the composition of the forest varies from place to place, there may be only one or two tree species in any particular area. It is too cold and the soil is too poor for trees to grow very tall. Many are no more than about 15 feet (4.6 m) high, and few rise to more than 35 feet (10.7 m).

A TAIGA ECOSYSTEM is much simpler than that of a broad-leaved deciduous forest. The coniferous trees provide food for birds, squirrels, and insects. They are hunted by predators such as owls, other birds of prey, and foxes.

Components of the ecosystem

1 Pine, spruce, fir, larch trees
2 Fallen cones, seeds, needles
3 Aphids, beetles
4 Red squirrel
5 Nutcracker
6 Bark beetle
7 Northern red-backed vole
8 Red ant in nest of pine needles
9 Pine grosbeak
10 Siberian tit
11 Western capercaillie
12 Goshawk
13 Pine marten
14 Gray owl
15 Dead vole
16 Red fox

Energy flow

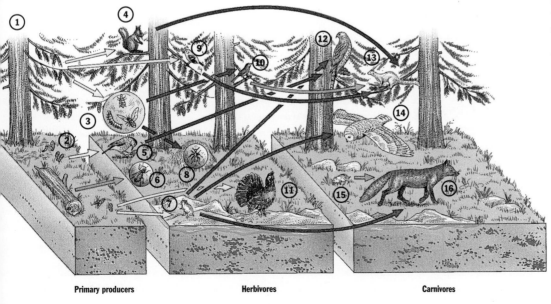

Primary producer/primary consumer

Primary/secondary consumer

Secondary/tertiary consumer

Dead material/consumer

Primary producers   **Herbivores**   **Carnivores**

Gymnosperms and Angiosperms

Conifers are plants that bear their seeds on woody scales grouped together to form cones. The word is from the Greek *konos,* meaning cone, and *phero,* meaning carry. Conifers form one of the major groups of plants, the division Coniferophyta; they are gymnosperms, a name derived from the Greek *gymnos,* "naked," and *sperma,* "seed," because they produce seeds that are not enclosed in an ovary. Gymnosperms first appeared about 465 million years ago.

The other major group of plants, the angiosperms, evolved much later. The name is derived from the Greek *angion,* meaning container, because angiosperms produce seeds that are contained in an ovary. The earliest angiosperm appeared more than 120 million years ago.

Gymnosperms and angiosperms differ in the way they produce seeds. In gymnosperms a male, or pollen, cone produces hundreds of tiny capsules, called sporangia, that are held in small leaves ("sporophylls"). Cells in the sporangia divide to produce structures that develop into pollen grains.

A female, or ovulate, cone contains many scales, each of which bears two ovules. An ovule has a sporangium (which is called the nucellus) enclosed in a protective coat with a single opening, the "micropyle." Pollen released from the male cone is carried away by the wind. Some grains land on female cones. There a pollen grain is drawn through the micropyle into the ovule, where it germinates and grows a pollen tube. This pierces the nucellus and releases two sperm cells. Then the cells in the nucellus mature, one of them surviving to be fertilized. Fertilization usually takes place more than a year after the plant has been pollinated. After fertilization the resulting embryo—together with

BOG AND MUSKEG VEGETATION. Bog and wet peat soil (muskeg) cover large areas throughout the taiga. Trees and bushes grow on the muskeg. On still wetter ground there are other plants, the remains of which contribute to peat formation. Pools become covered with bog mosses, with other plants growing on and among them. This changes the pools to bog.

Tamarack *(Larix laricina),* Labrador tea *(Ledum groenlandicum),* and dwarf juniper *(Juniperus communis var. depressa)* form forests on raised peat

Sedges and cattails *(Typha)* grow on the wet fern, and marsh marigolds *(Calla palustris)* may also be found

On gently sloping ground birch *(Betula pumila)* and a variety of peat-forming plants occupy low ridges of peat known as strings. Sedges *(Carex)* fill shallow pools between the ridges

Sedges, pitcher plants *(Sarracenia),* and bog mosses occupy the pools

a food supply—forms the seed, enclosed in a seed coat.

In an angiosperm the reproductive structure is a flower. Many species are pollinated by insects or other animals and have brightly colored or (to the pollinator) pleasantly scented flowers to attract them.

The ovules, which are fertilized after pollination, are contained in an ovary at the base of the flower. The seeds develop inside the ovary, which matures to become a fruit.

Gymnosperms and angiosperms also differ in the structure of their xylem cells. Those of gymnosperms are long, tapered cells called tracheids, which overlap at the ends. Those of angiosperms are shorter, wider, and joined end to end to form continuous tubes (see page 18).

WETLANDS OF THE TAIGA

Seen from the air, the dark green of the taiga is broken by innumerable ponds and lakes. There are also open areas that might be forest clearings or—more commonly—bogs.

There are many natural hollows in the ground in the far north. They were made by ice during the last ice age and have since filled with water. These are the lakes and ponds of the taiga. Trees cannot grow in them, and their banks receive more light than the forest floor. Smaller plants can grow there, provided their roots can tolerate the wet ground. Sedges (*Carex* species), cattails (*Typha* species), and pitcher plants (*Sarracenia* species) grow around the edges, and little by little bog mosses (*Sphagnum* species) spread out across the surface of the

water. As the layer of moss thickens and other plants grow in and among it, the pond is changed into bog.

Dead plant matter does not decay completely. Instead it forms peat, often as a series of ridges called strings. Trees such as junipers and tamarack (*Larix laricina*), together with shrubs such as Labrador tea (*Ledum groenlandicum*), establish themselves wherever

TAIGA FOREST in Kluane National Park in Yukon Territory, Canada. Here composed of spruce, pine, and fir, it provides a habitat for large mammals such as bears, caribou, and moose, but the animals are spread over a large area and are rarely encountered.

there is a sufficiently thick layer of peat, but the trees are usually small and stunted. Sedges (*Carex* species) are the commonest plants of the low-lying peat areas. This type of wetland is known as Carex fen. Fen peat is slightly alkaline or neutral. This distinguishes it from bog peat, which is acid.

BIRDS OF THE TAIGA

Parrots are the most famous birds of tropical forests. In the taiga there is a bird that lives in much the same way as a parrot, although it is much smaller and less well known. It is the crossbill, of which there are several species, all belonging to the genus *Loxia*. Crossbills are finches (family Fringillidae). They are slightly larger than sparrows, and their name refers to their broad bills, the tips of which are crossed.

Crossbills feed on the seeds of coniferous trees, using their bills like tweezers to extract the seeds from the cones. Like parrots, they spend most of their time high above the ground climbing about in the trees, often in groups. Once they have extracted the seeds from their cones, they drop the empty cones onto the ground; the presence of empty cones is clear evidence that crossbills have been feeding in the area.

The common, or red, crossbill (*Loxia curvirostra*) occurs in coniferous forests throughout the Northern Hemisphere, as does the smallest member of the genus, the white-winged crossbill (*L. leucoptera*). The parrot crossbill (*L. pytyopsittacus*) lives only in the Eurasian taiga.

There is also food for birds that forage on the ground. Turkeys (*Meleagris gallopavo*) live in North American forests. These are the ancestors of the domesticated gobbler. The bird was given its name by mistake. When British settlers first saw the American bird, they mistook it for a guinea fowl, which they called the turkeycock or turkeyhen because it was imported to Britain through the country of Turkey.

Turkeys eat berries and seeds, as well as invertebrate animals and small reptiles including snakes. Turkeys were hunted to such an extent that in the early part of this century they became very rare. Then they were protected, and their numbers have now recovered.

There are no wild turkeys in Eurasia, but there is an equivalent, the capercaillie (two species of *Tetrao*). They are the size of turkeys and feed on berries, grass, and the buds and young shoots of coniferous trees. The western capercaillie (*T. urogallus*) occurs throughout the taiga from Scotland and Scandinavia to central Siberia. It lives in those parts of the forests with dense undergrowth, but not too far from clearings and boggy areas, providing it with a variety of habitats in which to find food, shelter, and the open spaces on which the males display their fine plumage in the hope of attracting females. The black-billed capercaillie (*T. parvirostris*) is found only in eastern Siberia, mainly in larch forest but sometimes also in pine forests.

Capercaillies belong to the grouse family (Tetraonidae). There

THE GOSHAWK (*Accipiter gentilis*) (right) is the bird of prey most typical of the taiga. It occurs throughout North America and Eurasia. This one, in America, has caught a gray squirrel. Goshawks also hunt hares and ground-nesting birds and will chase pigeons through the forest.

Three-toed woodpecker
Picoides tridactylus

are also other grouse living in the taiga. The hazelhen or northern hazel grouse (*Tetrastes bonasia*), a bird about 14 inches (35 cm) long, is the most widespread. It is still hunted extensively in Russia. The larger Siberian spruce grouse (*Falcipennis falcipennis*) lives in the spruce, larch, and fir forests of southeastern Siberia.

Woodpeckers

Trees harbor many insects, including beetles that lay their eggs in crevices in the bark. When the eggs hatch, the larvae excavate tunnels for themselves just below the surface. Woodpeckers have evolved stiff tails to serve as props, bills as strong as chisels with which to chip open the bark, and long tongues with which to gather the grubs. Their skulls and brains are

WOODPECKERS *(below)* **are birds of temperate forests. They feed mainly on insects, but some also eat seeds and berries. The three-toed woodpecker lives in the coniferous forests of North America and Eurasia. The great spotted and green woodpeckers occur only in Europe and Asia, the green woodpecker preferring broad-leaved forests. The northern wryneck also lives in Eurasian broad-leaved forests.**

Great spotted woodpecker
Dendrocopos major

Northern wryneck
Jynx torquilla

Green woodpecker
Picus viridis

built to withstand the repeated shock of hammering at trees—a black woodpecker (*Dryocopus martius*) taps up to 12,000 times a day! They make up the family Picidae, and there are about 200 species of them. Theirs is obviously a highly successful way of life.

The great spotted woodpecker (*Dendrocopos major*) is the most widely distributed of the four species found in the Eurasian taiga. In addition to insects it eats seeds and berries. It occurs only in Europe and Asia, as does the black woodpecker, which is one of the biggest of all woodpeckers—about 18 inches (45 cm) long. The three-toed woodpecker (*Picoides tridactylus*) lives in both the North American and Eurasian taiga.

Birds of Prey

Small animals of the taiga are hunted mainly by owls, birds well adapted to forest life. One of the biggest owls in the world is the great gray owl (*Strix nebulosa*), some individuals being about 30 inches (76 cm) long. It inhabits the forests of both North America and Eurasia. The eagle owl (*Bubo bubo*), found only in Eurasia, is slightly smaller but much more heavily built.

Apart from owls, most birds of prey prefer open country. Sparrowhawks and their relatives in the family Accipitridae are the exception. The sparrowhawk (*Accipiter nisus*) lives in Eurasian forests and feeds on small birds, but the goshawk (*A. gentilis*) is the species most typical of the taiga. A large bird, up to 24 inches (61 cm) long, the goshawk occurs throughout North America and Eurasia. It feeds mainly on birds, which it chases and catches in flight, but also eats mammals, especially squirrels.

Elk, or wapiti
Cervus elaphus

Snowshoe hare
Lepus americanus

MAMMALS OF THE TAIGA

LARGE ANIMALS OF THE TAIGA include deer and hares and also formidable predators of the smaller species. The gyrfalcon often catches birds in flight. Hares are prey to lynxes, foxes, and other carnivorous mammals.

Squirrels are the animals most closely associated with the taiga, and they spend most of their time above ground and out of sight. The red squirrel (*Sciurus vulgaris*) lives in coniferous forests throughout Europe and Asia. It eats a wide variety of plant foods, but relies mainly on seeds

Gyrfalcon
Falco rusticolus

Lynx
Felis lynx

Squirrels live above ground; other small rodents live on the forest floor. The Siberian chipmunk (*Eutamias sibiricus*) is very similar to its American relative the eastern chipmunk (*Tamias striatus*). There are also several species of voles and mice.

Most hares live in open country, but two species prefer life in the taiga. One is the American snowshoe hare (*Lepus americanus*), the other the Eurasian species *L. timidus*, known as the mountain, Arctic, Irish, blue, and varying hare. Both species have brown fur in summer and white fur in winter.

Wapiti, or elk (*Cervus elaphus*), known in Europe as red deer, live in more open parts of the forest, especially near pools and bogs. Their favorite foods are rushes and sedges, plants of wet ground, but they also eat grass and the shoots of shrubs and trees. Stags will sometimes rear up on their hind legs and use their antlers to break off branches.

Hunters of the Taiga

All the small mammals are hunted by possibly the most versatile of all carnivores: the red fox (*Vulpes vulpes*). It lives everywhere, including cities, but the forest is its real home. The red fox competes for food with owls and other birds of prey, as well as with the lynx (*Felis lynx*).

Hares, rodents, ground-nesting birds, and even small deer are prey to the lynx—a big, stocky cat. The lynx stalks its prey or lies in wait for it, hidden among low vegetation.

it takes from tree cones. Its North American counterpart is the gray squirrel (*S. carolinensis*), although it prefers broad-leaved forest. Populations of this species were introduced to Britain and Ireland several times between 1876 and 1929, and the gray squirrel is now much commoner there than the native red squirrel. Gray squirrels are, however, absent from other parts of Europe and Asia.

THE GRIZZLY BEAR
(Ursus arctos) **is the biggest of all bears. A male can be more than 8 feet (2.4 m) tall. A subspecies of the brown bear, it is found in the northwest of North America and throughout the Eurasian taiga. Its numbers have been reduced by hunting, but there are still big grizzlies in the forest.**

There are even bigger cats hunting in the taiga. The range of the mountain lion, or puma (*F. concolor*), extends into the southern edges of the North American coniferous forest.

The taiga is also home to the wolf (*Canis lupus*). There are several subspecies of wolves—two in North America and eight or nine in Russia. Not all live in forests, and those that do prefer the more open areas, where they find it easier to run down their prey. They will take small mammals only when deer, their preferred prey, are scarce.

Giants of the Taiga

Wolves will hunt red deer, but they prefer the biggest of all the deer, the moose (*Alces alces*), known in Europe as the elk. Standing up to 90 inches (2.3 m) tall at the shoulder and weighing up to 1,750 lb (794 kg), the moose is the biggest of all deer. Apart from its size it is recognizable by its long, drooping muzzle.

In winter, when all the rivers and ponds are frozen, it feeds on woody plants, but the rest of the year it feeds mainly on aquatic plants, so it is often found near water. It swims well and wades into the water in search of food.

The other giant of the taiga is the animal known in North America as the grizzly and in Europe as the brown bear (*Ursus arctos*). There are several subspecies distributed throughout the northwestern part of the North American boreal forest and throughout all of the Eurasian taiga. They vary in size, but grizzlies can be huge. In British Columbia and Alaska males can reach a length of 9 feet (2.7 m) from nose to tail and weigh up to 450 lb (204 kg). The bears of eastern Siberia are of similar size.

They eat both plant and animal food, and are very selective in choosing it. Bears enjoy being in water and will fish for salmon and trout with their teeth or paws. They also dig up plant tubers and eat berries, and will eat rodents, young deer, and farm livestock as well if the opportunity occurs.

People have been hunting bears for a very long time, and this greatly reduced their numbers. Hunting is now controlled throughout the taiga, and the bears will not disappear.

TREES OF THE TAIGA

Spruces occupy nearly 300,000 square miles (777,000 sq. km) of the Eurasian taiga, pine trees about 445,000 square miles (1,152,500 sq. km), and larches more than 1,000,000 square miles (2,590,000 sq. km). Several species of each of these are also widespread in the coniferous

forests of North America. There are also hemlocks (*Tsuga* species) in North America and in southern China and Japan. In North America they grow naturally in the northwest, from California to British Columbia, and in the east from the Great Lakes to the Atlantic coast. Hemlocks are widely cultivated elsewhere, as are all the trees of the conifer forests. In all, there are 34 species of spruce, 93 of pine, nine of larch, and ten of hemlock.

Spruces (*Picea* species) and firs (*Abies* species) have dense foliage, so the floors of spruce and fir forests are deeply shaded. The trees themselves can tolerate the shade, but few other plants grow in the near darkness. Most of the plants that do grow there produce white or very pale flowers, making them stand out against the darkness around them.

The trees themselves grow tall and straight. They are capable of attaining a height of about

MOOSE (*Alces alces*) are the biggest of all deer; the antlers of the male or bull can measure up to 6 feet (1.8 m) from tip to tip. This bull is feeding in the Denali National Park, Alaska. Moose live in the coniferous forest of North America and Eurasia.

160 feet (49 m), and spruces will grow in cold, wet ground. These features make them attractive to commercial growers, and both are widely cultivated in plantations.

Pine (*Pinus* species) and larch (*Larix* species) forests are much lighter and more open. Pines and larches prefer well-drained, fairly dry soil, although pines will tolerate a wider range of soil conditions than larches. Larches do not grow well on ground that is waterlogged, especially if it is wet in winter, when the water is likely to freeze. Pines have an open structure that allows light to penetrate, and larches (unusual among coniferous trees) are deciduous, so shed their leaves in fall, which lets light through. Consequently an abundance of smaller plants thrives on the floor of pine and larch forests.

In spring larches produce fresh new needles, pale green in color. These darken through the summer; in the fall they turn yellow or golden before being shed. The contrasting colors produced by a scattering of larches among the constant dark green of the pine trees makes a pine-larch forest very beautiful.

Hemlocks are sometimes called hemlock spruces because of their similarity to spruces, though most are somewhat smaller.

Douglas firs belong to the genus *Pseudotsuga*, which means "false hemlock." There are only four species, found in the western United States, central and eastern China, and Japan. Most are fairly small, but the Gray or Oregon Douglas fir or Oregon pine (*P. douglasii*) can grow to 330 feet (100 m). In 1895 a specimen 436 feet (133 m) tall was felled in British Columbia. Douglas firs are related to the spruces, and both belong to the pine family (Pinaceae).

Tamarack
Larix laricina

European larch
Larix decidua

Noble fir
Abies procera

White pine
Pinus strobus

Scots pine
Pinus sylvestris

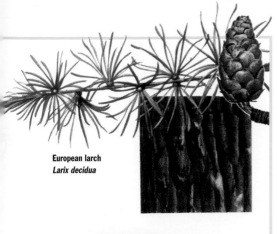

European larch
Larix decidua

Sitka spruce
Picea sitchensis

Norway spruce
Picea abies

Douglas firs require well-drained soils. They thrive especially well on the sides of valleys.

THE NORTHERN BROAD-LEAF

In the far north, where the coniferous forest gives way to tundra, there are shrubs seldom more than 40 inches (100 cm) tall. These are dwarf birch (*Betula nana*), the most northerly of all broad-leaved tree species for, despite its small size, the dwarf birch is a tree.

Birches—about 60 species in the genus *Betula*—produce large amounts of seed that are dispersed by the wind. The seed germinates readily and the trees grow quickly. Consequently, if bare ground is left untended, the first trees to appear in it are often birches. Birch trees are not long-lived, however. While they live, the seeds of other species germinate, and when the birches die, these later arrivals grow up, shading out birch seedlings. So birches appear on open ground, but later they disappear.

This does not occur in the far north, however, because other broad-leaved trees cannot survive there. Without competitors to shade them, the birches thrive.

They are handsome trees with a particularly attractive bark. The lenticels— slit-like pores through which gases enter and leave the trunk or branch—are horizontal and clearly visible as thin, dark lines. The bark is often silvery or white, although in some species it is yellow, red, or black. The most abundant Eurasian species, which also grows in North Africa, is the silver birch (*B. pendula*), which has white bark. The

FIR, PINE, SPRUCE, AND LARCH *(opposite)* **are among the commonest kinds of tree in the taiga, and there are several species of each. Hemlocks occur naturally in the west and east of North America, and in southern China and Japan, but not in the Eurasian taiga. Larches are deciduous. Their young needles are pale green. These darken through summer, and turn yellow and golden in fall, before being shed.**

downy birch (*B. pubescens*) also has white bark, but the paper birch (*B. papyrifera*) of North America has the whitest bark of all. The paper birch is also known as the canoe birch. Some Native American peoples used to collect sheets of bark from this tree and fasten them together over a wooden frame to make birchbark canoes. They waterproofed the skin with Canada balsam, resin from the balsam fir (*Abies balsamea*).

Birches have found traditional uses in most northern cultures, perhaps because they can be found where no other broad-leaved tree can survive. The wood is used to make furniture and a variety of utensils, including a type of broom called a besom.

Aspens and Alders

The 35 species of poplars, aspens, and cottonwoods all belong to the genus *Populus*. They are related to willows in the family Salicaceae and occur throughout the Northern Hemisphere south of the tundra.

Aspens seem to tremble in the slightest breeze. The effect is due to their leaf stalks (petioles), which are long and flattened; when the wind catches the leaves, they sway, and the simultaneous swaying of all the leaves makes the entire tree appear to quake. This is reflected in the names. The European aspen is *Populus tremula* and the quaking aspen of North America is *P. tremuloides* (both derive their names from the Latin word for quivering, which is *tremulus*).

Alders (*Alnus* species) are trees found on wet ground, often on wet peat soil in areas known as fens. A stand of alders growing in a fen is called a carr, although nowadays the term is often applied to fen woodland regardless of

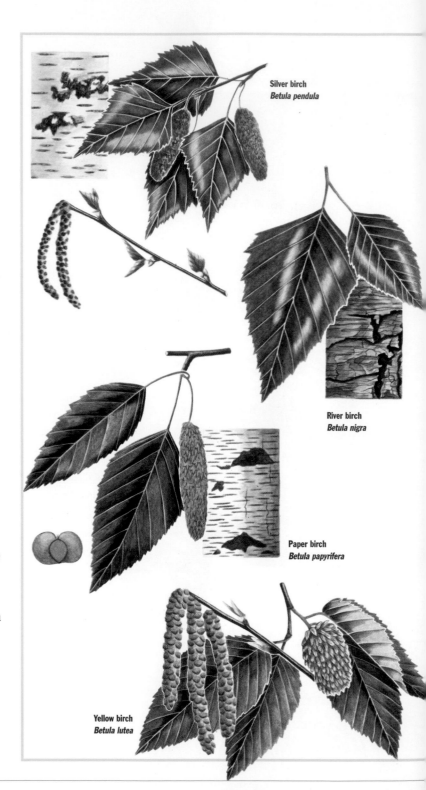

Silver birch
Betula pendula

River birch
Betula nigra

Paper birch
Betula papyrifera

Yellow birch
Betula lutea

Gray alder
Alnus incana

Aspen
Populus tremula

Hornbeam
Carpinus betulus

which species it includes. Alders are not difficult to recognize because their seeds are produced in woody fruits that look very like small pine cones, the tree retaining the cones long after the seeds have been shed.

In forests, alders grow along the banks of rivers and near ponds and lakes. Their presence enriches the soil, because alders have nodules on their roots containing colonies of bacteria. These bacteria (the species is *Frankia alni*) convert atmospheric nitrogen into a compound the tree can use in the manufacture of proteins. When an alder tree dies, this nitrogen enters the soil to be recycled.

Because wood from the alder is resistant to rotting when wet, it was used traditionally to make wooden shoes, called clogs.

LIFE FARTHER SOUTH

Birches, aspens, and alders are deciduous trees. They shed all their leaves each fall and grow new ones each spring. The new leaves must open quickly and as early as possible so that the trees can start the process of photosynthesis and growing without delay, but to achieve this they must produce their leaf buds while the weather is still cold. Sharp frosts can destroy the delicate buds, however, so the trees can grow only where severe spring frosts are very unusual.

Coniferous trees do not face this problem because they are evergreen, retaining their leaves throughout the year. They, too, must produce new leaves from buds because after a year or two individual leaves grow old and die, but they can do so at any time of year because they do

BIRCH, ASPEN, AND ALDER *(opposite)* grow in the far north. Birches will grow on the very edge of the forest, where trees give way to tundra, and even grow in southern Greenland. Aspens also grow throughout the taiga. Alders prefer wetter sites and are often found near pools and on river banks.

WAPITI, ELK, OR RED DEER *(Cervus elaphus)* **occur throughout the temperate regions of the Northern Hemisphere. They prefer to live in the boundary between forest and open grassland, and are often found in forest clearings. Only the stags (males) have antlers.**

not have to replace all their leaves at the same time. Nor do coniferous trees have to expend nutrients growing a new set of leaves altogether.

The leaves themselves are different. Those of coniferous trees are reduced to needles or scales and have a thick, waxy outer skin. This minimizes the loss of water from the tree, helping the tree survive the winter when there is no liquid water for its roots to absorb.

Deciduous trees must use nutrients growing their leaves, but the trees are economical: before leaves are shed in the fall, most of the nutrient substances they contain move back into the tree, where they are stored through the winter. The leaves are thinner and flimsier than conifer needles or scales—they do not need to last so long—but they are much bigger, which is why these trees are called broad-leaved.

Not all broad-leaved trees are deciduous—holly and some species of oak are among the broad-leaved evergreens—but most are. Those that are evergreen have tough, waxy leaves to reduce water loss, and they grow mainly in places with a hot, dry summer. There are also a few deciduous conifers, such as larches and the dawn redwood (*Metasequoia glyptostroboides*). Shedding their leaves allows these trees to shut down completely in winter; because they do not have to last so long, their leaves are less robust than those of most coniferous trees.

Life in the Broad-Leaved Forest

During winter the trees in the broad-leaved forest are bare. Sunlight penetrates to the forest floor. The ground is cold and may be covered with snow, but between the melting of the snow and thawing of the ground and the emergence of leaves on the trees there is a time when the ground is warmed by the sunshine of early spring. Flowering herbs have adapted to take advantage of this opportunity. In the few weeks available to them, they flower—often with bright colors to attract the insects that pollinate them—and set seed. Then the trees produce their leaves, the canopy closes above them, and the forest floor is plunged into dappled shade.

Even in the depth of winter only the surface layer of the soil freezes, and it does not remain frozen for long. The rest of the year the ground is moist, but not waterlogged, so plants can grow over most of the forest floor. In clearings, produced naturally when a tree falls and brings one or two others down with it, grasses grow in full sunlight. Grasses cannot tolerate shade, so at the edge of the clearing, the grass-covered area gives way to shade-loving plants and mosses.

Leaves, which are shed each fall, form a layer on the forest floor. They and the living plants provide food and shelter for small animals. Wherever there are small, plant-eating animals there are larger animals hunting them.

AN ECOSYSTEM IN A BROAD-LEAVED DECIDUOUS FOREST is more complex than that in a coniferous forest. Leaves are shed each year, and unlike pine needles, they decompose quickly and easily. This provides food for soil organisms and the small animals living on the forest floor.

Components of the ecosystem

1 Oak trees, fruits, leaf litter
2 Herbivorous insects
3 Insects
4 Long-tailed field mice, bank voles
5 Earthworms
6 Wild boar
7 Gray squirrel
8 Great tit
9 Sparrowhawk
10 Spider
11 Green woodpecker
12 Tawny owl
13 Badger
14 Weasel
15 Mole

Energy flow

⇨ Primary producer/ primary consumer
➡ Primary/secondary consumer
⇨ Secondary/tertiary consumer
➡ Dead material/ consumer
➡ Death

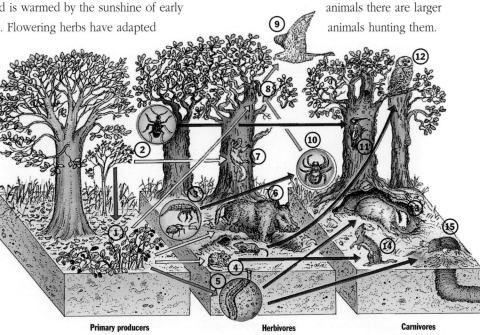

Primary producers   **Herbivores**   **Carnivores**

Despite their name, pine martens (*Martes martes*) prefer deciduous forest or mixed forest that has both broad-leaved and coniferous trees to purely coniferous forest. They feed on small birds, rodents, and invertebrate animals. Weasels (*Mustela nivalis*) also prefer woodland, especially in winter, but will live anywhere they can find the mice and voles that are their main food. They are tiny carnivores, rarely more than about 9.5 inches (24 cm) long including the tail. Badgers are also members of the weasel family (Mustelidae). The Eurasian badger (*Meles meles*) feeds on small animals, including rabbits, rats, mice, beetles and other insects, as well as fruit, nuts, seeds, roots, and grass, but worms are its favorite and chief food. It lives in broad-leaved forests. The American badger (*Taxidea taxus*) prefers dry grassland.

ON THE FOREST FLOOR

Dead leaves, branches, and the waste products and remains of all the plants and animals of the forest accumulate on the forest floor. This layer of material is called litter. All this organic material provide food for another community of forest dwellers. Mostly unseen, they live among the litter and below ground in the upper layer of the soil.

Each member of the community has its own way of life, so they all live

and feed differently and do not compete. Slugs and snails eat only soft leaves. Slugs, lacking shells to protect them, must remain among these moist leaves. In contrast, snails can climb trees, grazing on the tiny plants called algae that grow on the bark.

Earthworms eat decaying plant material and also soil. They are active only when they are wet, but if they become dry, they can survive motionless for weeks or even months, reviving once they are wet again. In a temperate forest there are usually hundreds of worms beneath every square yard (sq. m) of the surface—they are less common in the subtropics and tropics.

Most millipedes eat decaying plant material, although some prefer living plants, and some eat fungi. Some centipedes eat decaying plant material, but most are carnivores, hunting animals smaller than themselves.

Termites are able to eat wood and other tough plant material, although some termite

ON THE FOREST FLOOR there is a large community of animals and fungi feeding in the layer of dead plant and animal matter. After these organisms have eaten the material, their own wastes are food for bacteria. Eventually the organic matter is converted into simple chemical compounds that can pass into plant roots to be used again. Some of the animals, such as earthworms, drag leaves and other items below the surface.

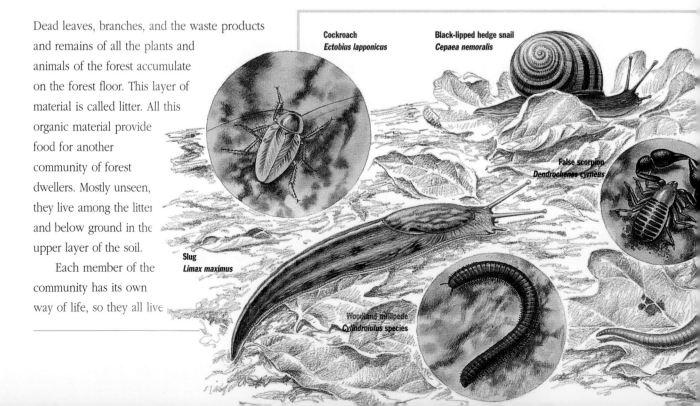

Cockroach
Ectobius lapponicus

Black-lipped hedge snail
Cepaea nemoralis

False scorpion
Dendrochernes cyrneus

Slug
Limax maximus

Woodland millipede
Cylindroiulus species

species feed on fungi that they cultivate. Depending on the species, they live in galleries and chambers they excavate in dead wood, in colonies below ground, or in mounds built from sand and clay.

There are many species of insects. Beetles live on the surface or just beneath it. There are the larvae of flies, some of which feed on dead animals. Ants are very numerous, and there are many species. Some feed on plants, some on fungi, and some hunt other insects. False scorpions, or pseudoscorpions, are tiny, few being more than 0.3 inch (7.6 mm) long, so they are rarely seen despite being very common. They feed on springtails and mites. Springtails are tiny insects, most less than 0.04 inch (1 mm) long, that feed on bacteria, fungi, and spores.

Mites are about the same size as springtails. They feed on a variety of foods. Some mites are carnivorous, preying on nematodes—wormlike animals that are even smaller.

Together, these and all the other small animals that live on and in the soil contribute to the breaking down of organic material by digesting it and excreting what they are unable to digest. Their wastes provide food for bacteria, which complete the process of decomposition.

AIRBORNE IN THE FOREST

Squirrels are not the only forest-dwellers to store food. Most members of the crow family (Corvidae) also do so. Nutcrackers—relatives of crows—specialize in hoarding seeds from

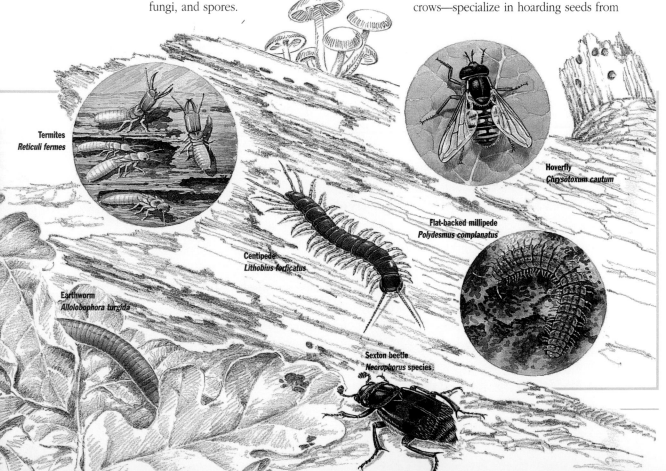

Termites
Reticuli fermes

Hoverfly
Chrysotoxum cautum

Flat-backed millipede
Polydesmus complanatus

Centipede
Lithobius forficatus

Earthworm
Allolobophora turgida

Sexton beetle
Necrophorus species

coniferous trees and nuts from broad-leaved trees. Their young hatch in March and April, and the birds have been seen feeding them on nuts they must have stored the previous fall.

There are two species of nutcrackers. The nutcracker (*Nucifraga caryocatactes*) lives in central and northern Europe and northern Asia. It is very similar to Clark's nutcracker (*N. columbiana*), which lives in the western United States. Both are about 12 inches (30 cm) long, live and feed in the same way, but are different colors. This similarity is repeated in many of the groups of birds inhabiting temperate forests. It is not surprising: the forests on either side of the Atlantic provide similar opportunities and challenges.

Broad-leaved forests change with the seasons. This means the food supply for birds also changes, so many birds eat different foods at different times. Tits—the name is short for titmice—are a good example. Insects are their main food and the young are always fed on insects, especially caterpillars. Later in the year, however, when fruits are abundant and insects less so, tits will eat berries and seeds. Most species of tits nest in hollow trees, but old and unhealthy trees with suitable holes are usually removed in managed forests and plantations.

There have been many scientific studies of tits and the way they live. One study, made in 1960 in Dutch woods by the Nobel Prizewinning zoologist Nikolaas Tinbergen (1907–88), revealed just how many insects they eat and the effect they have in controlling them. Now foresters encourage them by providing nesting boxes.

Tits occur worldwide, wherever there are trees. In North America some species are known

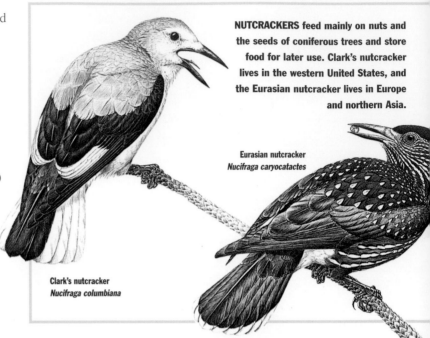

NUTCRACKERS feed mainly on nuts and the seeds of coniferous trees and store food for later use. Clark's nutcracker lives in the western United States, and the Eurasian nutcracker lives in Europe and northern Asia.

Eurasian nutcracker
Nucifraga caryocatactes

Clark's nutcracker
Nucifraga columbiana

as chickadees, a name based on their song. They are all very similar. Most "true" tits belong to the genus *Parus* in the family Paridae. Long-tailed tits and penduline tits make up the families Aegithalidae and Remizidae. *Parus* is the genus that includes some of the most familiar tits, such as the black-capped chickadee (*P. atricapillus*) of Canada and the northern United States.

Hunters of the Air

Caterpillars feed on the leaves of trees, and blue tits feed on caterpillars. Blue tits are hunted by sparrowhawks (*Accipiter nisus*). In North America black-capped chickadees often fall prey to the sharp-shinned hawk (*A. striatus*) or Cooper's hawk (*A. cooperii*). The sparrowhawk and the sharp-shinned hawk are both up to about 14 inches (35 cm) long. Cooper's hawk is slightly bigger.

Sparrowhawk
Accipiter nisus

Sharp-shinned hawk
Accipiter striatus

Blue tit
Parus caeruleus

Azure tit
Parus cyanus

Again, related species live and behave in very similar ways in North American and Eurasian forests. These birds and the goshawks belong to the same genus. They are typical bird hawks (hawks that hunt birds). A study of the behavior of Cooper's hawks lasting 5 years (1948–53) found that 82 percent of their diet consists of small birds, the remainder being made up of small mammals, principally chipmunks and squirrels.

Bird hawks nest in trees. The sharp-shinned hawk usually prefers coniferous trees, although it will nest in alders and sycamores (*Platanus occidentalis*, also known as the buttonwood and buttonball; the tree known in Britain as the sycamore is *Acer pseudoplatanus*, a quite different species). The sparrowhawk also prefers conifers, especially spruce. Cooper's hawks usually nest in sycamore trees.

Bird hawks use the same hunting technique. They first spend some time circling slowly, high above the forest, to locate an area in which prey is abundant. Then they enter the area they have identified and wait for prey to come within range. The hawk sits quite still and silent on a branch, sometimes in full view and sometimes partly hidden behind foliage. When prey appears, the bird launches itself into the air, dropping with its wings partly folded or flying in swift pursuit.

OAKS AND ELMS

Oak symbolizes strength and durability. Its wood is highly prized for its handsome appearance as

BIRDS OF THE TEMPERATE FORESTS of North America and Eurasia live in similar ways and consequently resemble one another. Tits occur in both the Old and New Worlds, but the species are different. The blue tit is found throughout Europe and the azure tit in Russia and northern China. The sparrowhawk lives in Eurasia, and the sharp-shinned hawk in North and South America.

well as its reliability. From about 1550, when the English were building ships for trading and for war, oak was used for everything except the masts. It remained a favored timber in shipbuilding until the middle of the 19th century.

The reputation of oak is certainly deserved. The two English species are the common oak (*Quercus robur*) and the durmast or sessile oak (*Q. petraea*). Both species supplied timber for shipbuilding. These are classed as "white" oaks. Several American species are at least as valuable. White oak (*Q. alba*), a tree up to 150 feet (45 m) tall, and the burr oak (*Q. macrocarpa*), which can reach a height of 170 feet (52 m) and has a trunk up to 7 feet (2 m) in diameter, also produce very valuable timber. "Red" oaks are not quite so tough, but several species are important sources of greatly prized wood. Red oak (*Q. rubra*) is probably the best known. Its small branches have dark-red bark.

Most oaks are deciduous, but not all. Those species that grow naturally in climates with a hot, dry summer are evergreen. Live oak (*Q. virginiana*) grows in the southern United States and Mexico and is evergreen. It is said to produce the most durable of all oak timber. Holm or holly oak (*Q. ilex*) is an evergreen oak that grows naturally around the shores of the Mediterranean. Its name comes from its pointed leaves, which resemble those of the holly.

Altogether there are about 600 species of oaks, all in the genus *Quercus*. They are found

Summer

Fall

Red oak
Quercus rubra

Common oak
Quercus robur

Durmast oak
Quercus petraea

Common oak
Quercus robur

Red oak
Quercus rubra

Chinese elm
Ulmus parvifolia

American elm
Ulmus americana

English elm
Ulmus procera

throughout the temperate regions north of the equator. They have many uses. Cork, for example, is obtained from the cork oak (*Q. suber*) of southern Europe and North Africa. Its cork layer is unusually thick, and the cork is harvested without harming the tree.

Decline and Disease

Elms (*Ulmus* species) are found in eastern North America, Europe, and eastern Asia. They are very widespread in China.

When broad-leaved forest established itself in northern Europe following the last ice age, elm was an important component. Elm pollen is very common in soils that can be dated to that time, but in soils dated at around 5,000 years ago there is a large and abrupt reduction. Scientists call this the "elm decline." Although there is not the slightest doubt that elm decline happened, no one really knows why. There are several possible explanations, however, of which two are the most likely. Either the trees died in an outbreak of disease, or they were severely disturbed or even destroyed by farmers.

At the time of the decline people had started growing cereal crops and keeping cattle. They must have made clearings in the forest in which to grow their crops, and in winter they probably kept their cattle corralled and brought their food to them. Cattle enjoy eating the leaves of trees, especially elm, so farmers may have cut off elm branches and stored them for use in winter. If that is what happened, they would have removed the elm flowers with the branches, so although the trees were not seriously harmed, they would have been prevented from producing pollen, which

OAKS AND ELMS
(opposite) **are the most famous trees of the broad-leaved deciduous forests, although in this century the number of elms has been greatly reduced by Dutch elm disease. Both trees are important sources of timber. For three centuries, from the time of the Spanish Armada to the Napoleonic wars and Trafalgar, timber from English oaks (the common oak and durmast or sessile oak) was used to build merchant and naval ships. Elm was valued because the wood does not split easily, and it does not rot if it is permanently sodden.**

might account for the reduction in the amount of pollen in the soil.

Another possibility is that the trees could have succumbed to an outbreak of Dutch elm disease. There have been many such outbreaks. An epidemic starting in the 1920s killed many American elms; in the 1960s there was a devastating epidemic in Europe that killed 25 million of the 30 million elm trees in Britain.

It is called "Dutch" elm disease because it was in the Netherlands that the organism responsible was first identified, in 1919. The disease is caused by a fungus, *Ophiostoma ulmi*, that blocks xylem vessels and is spread by beetles. These burrow into the bark, taking fungal spores with them.

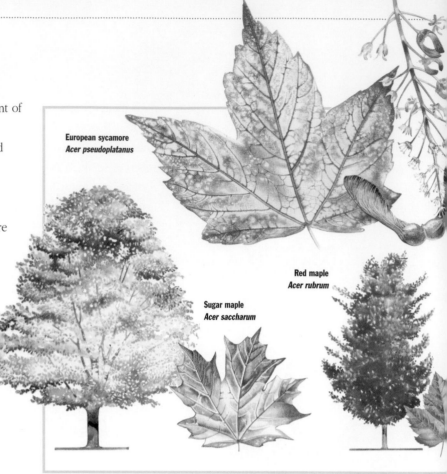

European sycamore
Acer pseudoplatanus

Sugar maple
Acer saccharum

Red maple
Acer rubrum

COLORS OF FALL

Deciduous forests change their appearance through the year. In winter the branches of the trees are bare, in spring the trees have new leaves that are bright green, in summer the leaves darken, and in the fall the trees present a brilliant patchwork of yellows, reds, and browns.

Maples (*Acer* species) produce the most spectacular fall colors, and some species are cultivated for their attractive foliage. In eastern North America, for example, the green leaves of the sugar maple (*A. saccharum*) turn bright orange or scarlet in the fall, and the red maple (*A. rubrum*) has yellow, orange, red, and purple fall leaves all on the same tree. The most widespread European maples are less

sensational, but leaves on the field maple (*A. campestre*) turn yellow or purple before they are shed. Some cultivated varieties of the Japanese maple (*A. palmatum*) have dark red or purple leaves throughout the year.

Beech trees (*Fagus* species) also produce beautiful fall colors. One cultivated variety of the common European beech (*F. sylvatica forma purpurea*) has leaves that are dark red, purple, or almost black. Larches (*Larix* species) are conifers and unusual in being deciduous. They also change color, their needles turning yellow or golden before they drop.

In fact, the leaves of all deciduous trees change color before they are shed at the end of the growing season. The change results from the way deciduous plants prepare for winter.

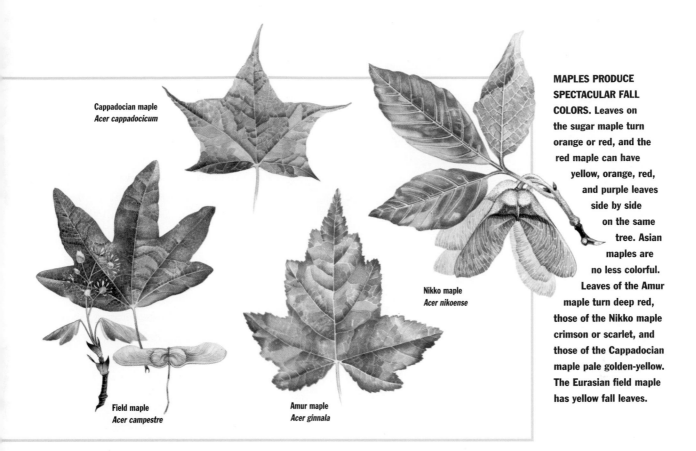

Cappadocian maple
Acer cappadocicum

Nikko maple
Acer nikoense

Field maple
Acer campestre

Amur maple
Acer ginnala

MAPLES PRODUCE SPECTACULAR FALL COLORS. Leaves on the sugar maple turn orange or red, and the red maple can have yellow, orange, red, and purple leaves side by side on the same tree. Asian maples are no less colorful. Leaves of the Amur maple turn deep red, those of the Nikko maple crimson or scarlet, and those of the Cappadocian maple pale golden-yellow. The Eurasian field maple has yellow fall leaves.

When Leaves Are Shed

By late summer the days are growing shorter and the nights longer. Deciduous plants sense this change in the hours of daylight and are also sensitive to the steady drop in temperature that heralds the coming of winter. When a deciduous plant detects these changes, chemical signals within the plant cause nutrients held in the leaves to move into the main part of the plant, where they are stored until it is time to return them to the new leaves the following spring.

The leaves stop making chlorophyll. This is the substance that captures sunlight, absorbing its energy to make sugars in the process known as photosynthesis. Chlorophyll is dark green, so as its level decreases, the leaves lose their green color. Other colors present in the leaves (but usually masked by the strong color of chlorophyll) then start to show. These include anthocyanins, a group of compounds present in sap that are red, blue, or violet in color.

There are also compounds called xanthophylls. These are present in leaf cells and help in photosynthesis by absorbing light energy at wavelengths to which chlorophyll does not respond. They are called accessory pigments and are produced by oxidizing another group of substances called carotenoids. Different xanthophylls are red, orange, or yellow—they are what give tomatoes and carrots their color.

The precise color of each leaf depends on the proportions in which these pigments are mixed. A leaf can be any shade of yellow, orange, red, purple, or brown.

FIRE IN THE CHAPPARAL.
Fire destroys the woody shrubs and also burns the substances the shrubs produce that poison other plants. Grasses and small herbs emerge rapidly, but before long the shrubs grow again and poison the plants around them.

The shedding of leaves is called abscission. There is a layer of cells, called the abscission layer, close to where the leaf stalk (petiole) joins the twig. Ethylene stimulates cells in the abscission layer to produce enzymes that break down the cell walls. A layer of cork is deposited on the side of the abscission layer nearest the twig, sealing off the connection between the plant and its leaf. After that the weight of the leaf, often helped by the wind, makes it fall.

TEMPERATE FORESTS IN DRY CLIMATES

In the western United States, and especially on the western side of the Sierra Nevada in California, and on dry slopes from Oregon to Baja California there is a type of vegetation known as chaparral. Similar vegetation is found in other parts of the world. Around the shores of the Mediterranean it is known as maquis in France, macchia in Italy, and matorral in Spain. It is also called matorral in Chile. In South Africa it is called Cape scrub or fynbos, and it is known as mallee scrub in Australia.

What these regions have in common is their climate. The rainfall is moderate, between 12 and 30 inches (300 and 760 mm) a year, but more than two-thirds of it falls in winter. Rainfall between May and October in the Northern Hemisphere and November to April in the Southern Hemisphere is usually less than 2 inches (51 mm), and in many places no rain falls at all in summer. Winters are mild. Temperatures rarely fall below freezing, and there are no severe frosts. Summers can be hot.

Summers are not dry enough nor winters cold enough to give any advantage to deciduous plants, so the trees and shrubs are broad-leaved

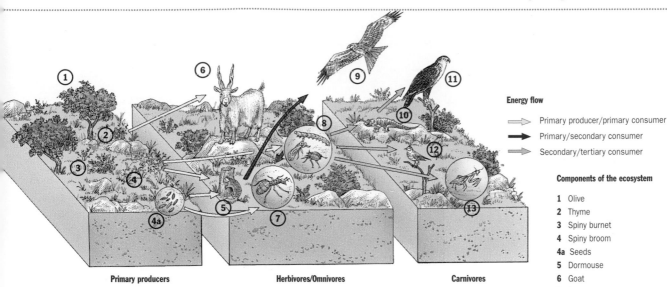

Energy flow

⟹ Primary producer/primary consumer
⟹ Primary/secondary consumer
⟹ Secondary/tertiary consumer

Components of the ecosystem

1 Olive
2 Thyme
3 Spiny burnet
4 Spiny broom
4a Seeds
5 Dormouse
6 Goat
7 Ants
8 Herbivorous insects
9 Red kite
10 Common gecko
11 Bonelli's eagle
12 Crested lark
13 Praying mantis

Primary producers   **Herbivores/Omnivores**   **Carnivores**

evergreens. In the chapparal they include Californian scrub oak (*Quercus dumosa*) and California lilac (*Ceanothus* species). Holm oak grows around the Mediterranean. The olive (*Olea europaea*) is one of the best-known trees

adapted to this type of climate. Apart from the trees, over much of the area dense thickets of shrubs grow up to about 10 feet (3 m) tall. In North America cacti grow among them.

The trees have small, hard leaves, often with sharp prickles around the edges, and thick bark. Their buds are protected beneath thick, waterproof scales. They usually have extensive lateral root systems as well as roots that reach deep below ground. These features all reduce the loss of water from the plant and help the plant absorb any moisture that is available. Trees and shrubs of this type are said to be sclerophyllous—literally "hard-leaved."

Fire

Many of the sclerophyllous plants produce oils, waxes, and a range of other chemical compounds. Some of these are poisonous to other plants, others prevent seeds from germinating, so they are able to exclude other plants from the soil they occupy. The compounds accumulate on the ground, and several of them are highly flammable. At the same time, as the woody plants grow older, they also accumulate dead, dry twigs and branches.

THE MAQUIS *(above)* **is a type of forest adapted to the mild winters and hot, dry summers of the Mediterranean region. Its evergreen trees and shrubs provide food for many species of insects and small mammals, which sustain reptiles and birds of prey.**

GARIGUE *(opposite)* **is a type of scrub vegetation that develops where chapparal or maquis is grazed too intensively or burned too often. The shrubs fill crevices in the rocks where soil accumulates and there is shade to lower the temperature. Many of the shrubs belong to the pea family (Leguminosae).**

TEMPERATE RAIN FOREST *(opposite)* develops where rainfall is high and spread evenly through the year, and temperatures are moderate. Like tropical rain forest, it supports luxuriant vegetation. This rain forest is in New Zealand. It contains southern beeches (*Nothofagus* species) and large numbers of tree ferns.

Under natural conditions at intervals of 30 to 40 years the vegetation in these dry climates catches fire. The fire burns fiercely, often reaching 1,200°F (649°C) at the surface. This kills many plants, leaving the soil bare and liable to erosion, but it also destroys the plant poisons. Grasses and herbs spring up and quickly cover the whole area. Within a few months some of the shrubs are producing shoots, but it is several years before all the trees and shrubs reestablish themselves.

In some areas fires have occurred more frequently than every 30 to 40 years, or grazing animals have consumed too much of the plant material, and the pattern has changed. The woody plants are smaller and more like scrub. This vegetation is called *garigue* in France, *phrygana* in Greece, and *tomillares* in Spain.

Australia and Its Gum Trees

Fires also occur at intervals in Australia. Its native trees, the eucalypts or gums (*Eucalyptus* species), are adapted to it. Some produce fireproof seeds that germinate after fire, but most have fireproof buds on their trunks from which new shoots grow.

Many eucalypts have a woody stem or root, called a lignotuber, lying on or just below the ground from which the main trunk grows. Some have a huge lignotuber and produce many stems. These many-stemmed varieties are called mallee, and they are characteristic of the Australian mallee scrub.

This is only one of their adaptations to the Australian climate. River red gums, such as *E. camaldulensis*, produce seeds that will germinate only after they have been thoroughly

EUCALYPTUS TREES are natives of Australia, with a few species from New Guinea, Mindanao in the Philippines, and some of the islands of Indonesia. They are now grown in most parts of the world for ornament and in the tropics as a source of timber. They are evergreen and include shrubs as well as some of the tallest trees in the world.

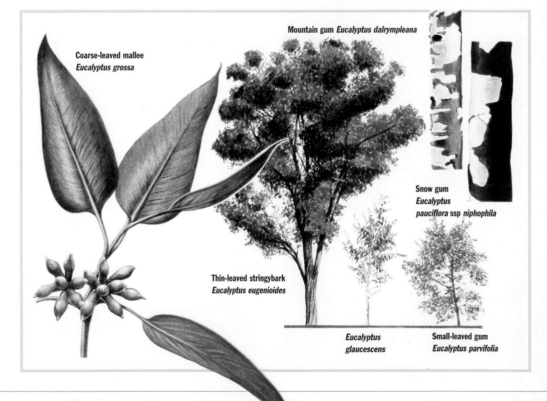

Coarse-leaved mallee
Eucalyptus grossa

Mountain gum *Eucalyptus dalrympleana*

Thin-leaved stringybark
Eucalyptus eugenioides

Snow gum
Eucalyptus pauciflora ssp *niphophila*

Eucalyptus glaucescens

Small-leaved gum
Eucalyptus parvifolia

soaked by a flood. The trees grow, age, and die, but new seedlings appear only after a flood. This may happen only a few times each century, but it is enough for the species to survive.

There are about 450 species of *Eucalyptus*. Some mallee species are no more than about 3.5 feet (1 m) tall, but the genus also includes the mountain ash (*E. regnans*—no relation to the European mountain ash). It grows to about 330 feet (100 m) and is the tallest flowering plant in the world (American redwoods are taller, but they are gymnosperms, not flowering plants).

Eucalypts are evergreen trees and shrubs that grow naturally only in Australia, New Guinea, Mindanao in the Philippines, and on some of the islands of Indonesia. As well as mallee scrub, they form forests. Wherever they grow, they are the biggest and most abundant plants. Many are of great commercial importance.

Jarrah (*E. marginata*) is a valuable timber tree, as are brown stringybark (*E. capitellata*), alpine ash (*E. delegatensis*), karri (*E. diversicolor*), and mountain ash. Karri, in particular, yields an extremely hard wood that resists attack by termites and other wood-boring pests. Many eucalypts are grown outside Australia, the most widely cultivated being the blue gum or fever tree (*E. globulus*), which has become naturalized in California. It is a source of eucalyptus oil.

FORESTS ON THE ROOF OF THE WORLD

In the eastern Himalayas, where the river known in Tibet as the Tsangpo and in India as the Brahmaputra cuts a deep channel through the mountains on its way south into Bangladesh and the sea, the lower slopes are cloaked in dense

CHERRY BLOSSOM in the forests covering the Yoshino Hills in Japan belongs to the Yoshino cherry *(Prunus yedoensis)*. This is a cultivated tree, as are all the Japanese flowering cherries. The blossoms soon fall, reminding Japanese people that life is short.

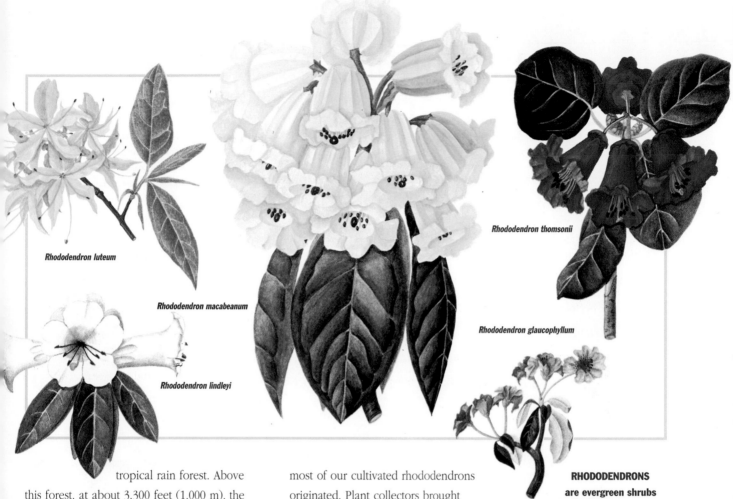

Rhododendron luteum

Rhododendron macabeanum

Rhododendron lindleyi

Rhododendron thomsonii

Rhododendron glaucophyllum

tropical rain forest. Above this forest, at about 3,300 feet (1,000 m), the forest becomes more temperate in type, with oaks and Asian chestnuts or chinquapins (*Castanopsis* species).

Then, at about 6,000 feet (1,830 m), this montane forest gradually starts changing into an upper montane forest. In spring this upper forest is ablaze with color. The trees and shrubs are rhododendrons; in the lower parts of the forest they grow alongside magnolias—which also have colorful flowers—and in the upper regions alongside fir and hemlock trees.

Rhododendrons grow naturally in several parts of the world, but more occur naturally in Asia than anywhere else, and especially in the Himalayas, which is the part of the world where most of our cultivated rhododendrons originated. Plant collectors brought specimens of many species to Europe and America during the last century, and the descendants of these plants are grown widely for ornament. In the Himalayas, though, the rhododendron forests, made up of many species, cover large areas.

Other Asian temperate forests are no less colorful. Some of those in Japan contain many kinds of flowering cherries. Admiring the cherry blossoms in early spring is a Japanese tradition with religious significance—the flowers are soon gone, reminding us how short life is. Most of the Japanese flowering cherries are cultivated varieties, carefully bred to produce the most beautiful and abundant flowers.

RHODODENDRONS are evergreen shrubs and small trees. They grow naturally in many parts of the Northern Hemisphere, but they originated in the Himalayas, where they form forests. The rhododendrons pictured above all grow in the Himalayas, except *R. luteum,* which grows in eastern Europe.

Survival of the Temperate Forests

*M*any centuries ago farmers cleared most of the natural forest that covered the lowlands of Europe. Native Americans cleared large areas of North American forest, and early European settlers cleared more. It might seem that the temperate forests were doomed to vanish, but they have survived. Their area is decreasing in Africa, Asia, and South America, but elsewhere new forests are being planted, and the total area of temperate forest is increasing.

Although the outlook for the increase of temperate forest is encouraging, the forests do not always consist only of healthy trees. In recent years there have been fears that large numbers of trees were succumbing to the effects of air pollution by "acid rain."

All rain is naturally slightly acid because gases such as carbon dioxide dissolve in water droplets and form acid solutions. Acid rain refers to rain that is more than naturally acid because it contains substances derived from gases released into the air from factory chimneys and the exhausts of cars and trucks. Rain, snow, drizzle, and fog that are acid are all called acid rain. Acids can also be deposited onto surfaces from dry air. This is called dry deposition.

From the 1970s onward there have been fears that acid rain has been killing large numbers of trees in central Europe, especially

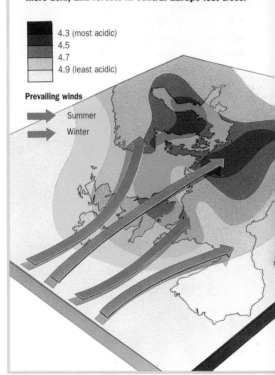

THE SPREAD OF ACID RAIN IN EUROPE. Taller smokestacks, installed in industrial regions to improve air quality by dispersing pollutants, allowed some pollutants to travel long distances. Lakes and soils in southern Norway and Sweden were made more acid, and forests in central Europe lost trees.

4.3 (most acidic)
4.5
4.7
4.9 (least acidic)

Prevailing winds

Summer

Winter

Germany. The Germans even invented a name for the phenomenon. They called it *Waldsterben*, "forest death." Later there were similar fears about the condition of North American forests.

POLLUTION AND "FOREST DEATH"

At first it was supposed that airborne sulfur dioxide was causing the trouble. When coal that contains sulfur is burned, the sulfur can be

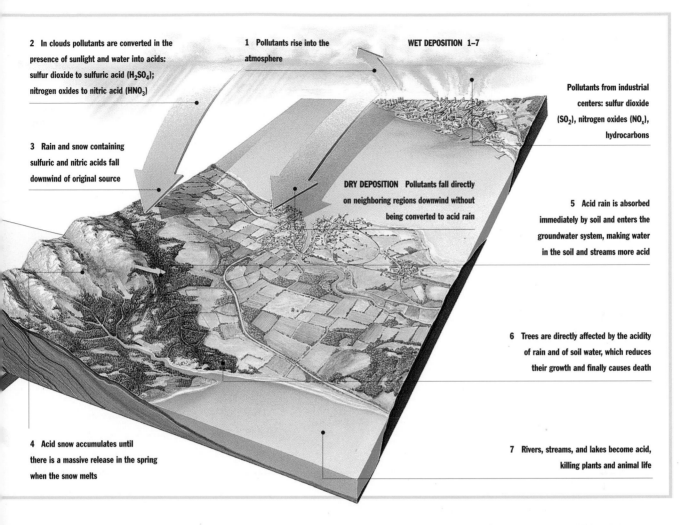

2 In clouds pollutants are converted in the presence of sunlight and water into acids: sulfur dioxide to sulfuric acid (H₂SO₄); nitrogen oxides to nitric acid (HNO₃)

1 Pollutants rise into the atmosphere

WET DEPOSITION 1–7

Pollutants from industrial centers: sulfur dioxide (SO₂), nitrogen oxides (NOₓ), hydrocarbons

3 Rain and snow containing sulfuric and nitric acids fall downwind of original source

DRY DEPOSITION Pollutants fall directly on neighboring regions downwind without being converted to acid rain

5 Acid rain is absorbed immediately by soil and enters the groundwater system, making water in the soil and streams more acid

6 Trees are directly affected by the acidity of rain and of soil water, which reduces their growth and finally causes death

4 Acid snow accumulates until there is a massive release in the spring when the snow melts

7 Rivers, streams, and lakes become acid, killing plants and animal life

released as sulfur dioxide (SO₂). In the air this reacts with hydroxyl (OH) in two steps, with sulfuric acid (H₂SO₄) as the end product. At low concentrations sulfur dioxide is harmless, or even beneficial, because sulfur is a plant nutrient, but at higher concentrations emissions of sulfur dioxide can damage trees. A copper smelter near Trail, British Columbia, opened in 1896 and emitted sulfur dioxide from then until 1930, and trees were damaged or killed for about 50 miles (80 km) downwind.

Sulfur dioxide was traveling long distances because an attempt to improve air quality had involved making industrial smokestacks taller. It was believed that the taller stacks would cause the gases to be much more diluted by the time they came into contact with anything they could damage.

Unfortunately, this did not work. Pollution levels fell near the factories, but there was very little reduction more than about 100 miles (161 km) away. In any case, sulfur was not the only

CHEMICAL REACTIONS in the air convert gases emitted by factories and traffic into acids. These can be transported long distances before eventually being deposited on surfaces or washed out of the air by precipitation.

culprit. In German forests measurements confirmed that sulfur levels were very low.

Ozone also came under suspicion. It, too, can damage trees, but experiments to determine whether it was a major cause of acid-rain damage were inconclusive. Nitrogen oxides emitted by factories and car exhausts may have caused harm. Reactions with rainwater convert them to nitric acid (HNO_3), which can poison plants, just as sulfuric acid can. Nitric acid is harmless in low concentrations, however, and nitrogen is an important plant nutrient.

Scientists began looking for less direct ways in which pollutants could harm trees. What they discovered were effects on the chemical

reactions that take place in the soil. When the water in the soil becomes more acid, magnesium and calcium attached to soil particles are replaced by hydrogen. The magnesium and calcium then enter the water and are carried away. Both of these are plant nutrients, and without them trees will not grow properly.

Rocks and clay contain aluminum. Most of it is securely bound in the compounds from which rocks and clay are made, but a small amount is loosely attached to soil particles from which it can be dislodged. Increasing acidity dislodges it, and then the aluminum becomes involved in other reactions that increase the soil acidity still more. This slows the rate at which organic matter decomposes, interfering with the recycling of nutrients. Aluminum can also enter root hairs, where it blocks the absorption of magnesium and calcium.

Other Causes of Damage to Forests

It was becoming apparent that the causes of damage were rather complex and involved more than just acid rain. In the early 1980s there was more concern when acid-rain damage seemed to be increasing rapidly in Europe. Beech trees (*Fagus sylvatica*) appeared to be badly affected.

This time acid rain was not the culprit, however. In 1976 there had been a severe drought in most of western Europe. This caused stress on trees that did not produce visible effects for several years; beech suffered more than most species because its roots are shallow, making it especially vulnerable.

During the 1970s German trees suffered from pest infestations and viral diseases. These were probably not a major cause of ill-health but

THE CAUSES AND EFFECTS OF ACID RAIN. Acid rain is only one cause of harm to forest trees. Much of the damage originally attributed to acid rain has since been found to be due to factors such as drought, disease, pest infestations, and nutrient deficiencies.

EFFECTS

Death

Tree weakened

Crown thinning

Leaf fall

Reduced resistance to disease, pests, and drought

Insufficient water

Nutrient deficiency

Water and nutrient uptake reduced

CAUSES

Acid rain

Direct damage to leaves

Acidification of soil

Direct damage to roots and release of poisonous chemicals from the soil

Soil nutrients washed out of soil

other plant nutrients has not changed. The trees grow bigger, but the growth is unbalanced because other nutrients are now in short supply compared with nitrogen; the trees are unable to harden their growing tips ready for winter and suffer severe frost damage. It is like a person who eats a lot and grows large, but whose diet contains far too little of one or more vitamins.

Weakening due to unbalanced growth caused by an excess of nitrogen is probably the reason for some of the tree damage. Industrial pollutants include nitrogen compounds, but in this case the nitrogen is believed to have come from farm livestock. Their urine contains nitrogen compounds that enter the soil, drain into the water below ground, and can then move from farms onto forest land.

Measuring the Damage

The first alarms were raised when foresters found that Norway spruce (*Picea abies*) trees were losing more than 10 percent of their needles. Commercially this is a very important species, especially in Germany, and one-third of the trees were thought to be damaged.

That diagnosis was wrong. Coniferous trees often lose more than 10 percent of their needles and soon recover. It is entirely natural. An internationally agreed definition of tree damage was drawn up in which less than 10 percent needle loss indicates no damage, 11–25 percent slight damage, 26–60 percent moderate damage, 61–98 percent severe damage. With more than 99 percent of its needles lost, a tree is dead. When this definition was applied to the German forests, the extent of the damage fell from more than half of the total forest area to less than one-fifth.

TREES CAN BE POISONED if they are directly exposed to concentrated pollutants. This happens to trees close to industrial centers. They can also be harmed indirectly if the soil becomes more acid, or if its balance of nutrients is altered.

would have weakened the trees, making them more susceptible to attack by acids or nutritional deficiencies.

Although nitrogen is essential for healthy growth, plants can suffer from having too much. Many forests grow on poor land where the soil contains less nitrogen than the trees could use. This deficiency restricts tree growth, and, if the supply of nitrogen increases, trees respond with a spurt of rapid growth. Although nitrogen has become abundant, however, the availability of

Signs of injury vary from one species to another. In the case of spruces a loss of 25 percent of its needles has no effect on the rate of growth.

Extent of the Problem

Forest trees do suffer damage and disease, but there are many causes. Signs of ill-health once attributed entirely to acid rain are now known to result from a number of quite different causes. Acid rain sometimes contributes to these, but most are entirely natural, and in time the forest recovers, even though some of its trees may die. Where the cause is the effect of acid rain on soil chemistry, however, recovery is often slow because of the time needed for the former chemical condition of the soil to be restored.

Governments have taken steps to reduce emissions, especially of sulfur dioxide. Indeed, emissions had already fallen substantially before the first reports of forest damage were made. Today, although acid rain continues to affect some lakes and rivers, it is no longer considered a serious problem in the forests of Europe and North America.

SCENT MARKING allows a giant panda to announce its presence and in the breeding season its gender and reproductive condition. Pandas live alone, and this is their principal means of communication. The scent is produced by glands beneath the base of the tail, which is used like a paintbrush to spread it at a prominent landmark.

ENDANGERED ANIMALS OF THE FOREST

Animals believed to be dangerous, or to take food from humans, have long been persecuted. At one time brown bears (*Ursus arctos*) inhabited European forests, but they are now confined to a few mountain areas in Spain, southwestern France, the Balkans, Scandinavia, and Russia. Hunting has also driven wolves out of much of the area they once occupied. Otters were hunted because they were believed to kill salmon and

trout. Birds of prey have been killed because they feed on birds that are hunted for sport. Although many species are now protected, not all are. People still hunt foxes, for example, often justifying their activity by exaggerating the harm they do to farmyard chickens and lambs.

Loss of Habitat

Hunting is not the main cause for the decline in certain animal species, however. Animals may escape the hunter, but there is no escape for the animal that loses its habitat. Clearing away the forest where it lives, then plowing the land to grow crops, robs it of shelter and food.

It seldom happens that entire forests are removed. More commonly, parts of the forest are cleared and converted to fields. Roads are built to provide access, and little by little, a single area of forest becomes many separate areas, like islands of forest in a sea of fields. A considerable total area of forest may remain, but it is fragmented, with forest animals isolated on these islands. Some find their island too small to provide them with the resources they need.

GIANT PANDAS *(Ailuropoda melanoleuca)*, **nowadays confined to forests in remote mountainous regions of western China, once lived in the lowlands and were much more numerous. Clearing the bamboo forests in which they live to provide farmland reduced their habitat and broke it into isolated fragments.**

1 **Young trees** eight to nine years old are thinned out in planted forests and frequently sold as Christmas trees

2 **After 30 to 40** years the lower branches start to drop off; the tree can be harvested for pulping

3 **At 50 to 60** years old the timber may be made into pulp, and straight trunks are used as poles

4 **At 100 years** old the tree can be cut for use as construction timber or "peeled" for plywood

5 **Growth slows** after 100 years, but the trunk is still used for timber. A mature tree may reach 325 feet (99 m)

6 **After several** centuries the tree starts to decline— the branches fall off, the bark peels, and the trunk begins to rot

7 **Even the upper** branches die in the end, and the rotten tree is so weak that...

8 **...it topples** to the ground

THE LIFE CYCLE OF THE DOUGLAS FIR ends after several centuries with the death of the tree. Douglas firs are widely grown in commercial plantations. There the trees are felled when they are about 50 or 60 years old—long before they grow sick and begin to die.

These animals disappear. Others can feed themselves but cannot find mates, so are unable to reproduce. They disappear too, but more slowly.

Scientists now recognize this kind of fragmentation as one of the most serious threats to wildlife. Projects to make new nature reserves or to alter existing areas of habitat now take account of this risk. Sometimes it may be best to leave a number of islands, but with lines of undisturbed habitat linking them, like roads. Alternatively, a single area the same size as those islands may be left undisturbed.

The Giant Panda

The most famous victim of habitat fragmentation is the giant panda (*Ailuropoda melanoleuca*), the animal that symbolizes wildlife conservation. At one time there were giant pandas living in lowland forests over much of western China. As more and more of the forest was cleared to provide land for farms, these large bears were pushed into the hills and finally into the mountains. The World Wide Fund for Nature estimates that the habitat for giant pandas was reduced by half between 1983 and 1998.

Today there are believed to be 1,000–1,500 giant pandas living wild. They are found only in the remotest parts of western China, in bamboo forests between 5,000 and 10,000 feet (1,500 and 3,000 m) high, in a total area of about 4,250 square miles (11,000 sq. km). Conservationists would like at least half this to be designated as a reserve to protect the remaining pandas.

LOGGING AND FORESTRY

Logging—the felling of trees for lumber—has never destroyed forests. Where trees are felled, new trees grow naturally to replace them, and the forest survives. Forests are destroyed only if the land they occupy is converted to another use. That use is always agriculture.

Today, the temperate forests of Eurasia and North America produce more than 70 percent of all the wood harvested throughout the world for industrial use and almost 80 percent of the wood that is made into paper and cardboard. The temperate forests are not decreasing in area, however. Between 1990 and 1995 those of North and Central America expanded by about 14,700 square miles (38,070 sq. km), those of Europe by about 7,500 square miles (19,425 sq. km), and those of the former Soviet Union by about 10,750 square miles (27,840 sq. km).

Timber production is now based almost entirely on the growing of trees as a crop. Newly planted forest plantations account for most of the increase in the forested area. Modern forestry aims to produce timber from the same land indefinitely, often by planting the forest initially, then allowing it to regenerate by itself after each

Weaker trees are felled to give more light and nutrients to the others

25 20 15
30   10
Years' growth

After the mature trees are felled, the branches are stripped and the trunks sawn into logs for transportation to the processing plant

Seeds are planted in a nursery where they grow to seedlings

Seedlings are planted out in the forest

harvest. This is usually more efficient and profitable than felling trees from natural forests, where the trees may be unhealthy and the required species widely scattered.

Not all the new forests are grown mainly for their lumber. Increasingly forests are regarded as environmental amenities. They support many species of wild plants and animals, and provide areas where people can relax and enjoy walking, cycling, or horseback riding. In Britain, for example, large areas of amenity forest, consisting of native broad-leaved deciduous trees, are being planted to serve urban population centers. In years to come it is probable that the temperate forests will continue to increase in size.

FOREST PLANTATIONS are tree farms on which trees are grown from seed, planted out, tended, and harvested when they reach a suitable size. Crops of trees can be produced indefinitely from a well-managed plantation, leaving the natural forest undisturbed.

Glossary

abscission The discarding of part of a plant, such as leaves in the fall.

alga A simple green plant that lacks true leaves, stem, and root. Many algae are single-celled; some are multicelled. Seaweeds are algae.

amphibian A vertebrate animal of the class Amphibia. The young develop in water, although the adults may live on land. Frogs, toads, newts, and salamanders are amphibians.

angiosperm A flowering plant in which the ovule bearing the seeds is enclosed within an ovary.

auxin One of several plant growth substances (sometimes called plant hormones, although their action is different from that of animal hormones) that is produced at the growing tips of stems and roots.

bark The outer "skin" of the trunk or branch of a tree. It is made up of a living inner layer of phloem cells (which transport sugars made by photosynthesis to all parts of the plant) and an outer layer of dead cork cells.

biome A large region throughout which living conditions for plants and animals are broadly similar, so the region can be classified according to its vegetation type.

boreal Meaning "of the north" and referring especially to the northern coniferous forest.

broad-leaved Having leaves with wide surfaces rather than leaves in the shape of needles or scales.

cambium A layer of cells that continues to divide throughout the life of a woody plant. The vascular cambium divides to produce phloem cells on one side and xylem cells on the other. The cork cambium (or phellogen) gives rise to cork cells on the outside and epidermal ("skin") cells on the inside.

carnivore An animal that feeds exclusively on other animals.

carotenoid Any of a group of red, orange, and yellow pigments found in cells in which photosynthesis occurs. They contribute to photosynthesis by absorbing light at wavelengths outside those absorbed by chlorophyll. There are two groups of carotenoids: carotenes and xanthophylls.

carr A wet habitat, with some peat in the soil, that is usually wooded, typically with alder (*Alnus*) or sometimes willow (*Salix*) species.

chlorophyll The green pigment, found in most plants, that absorbs light energy. This is then used to drive the reactions of photosynthesis.

climax The final stage in a plant "succession," in which the community of plants reaches a stable equilibrium in its environment.

conifer A gymnosperm tree or shrub in which the reproductive structures consist of separate male and female cones and the leaves are in the shape of needles or scales.

consumer An organism that is unable to manufacture its own food from simple ingredients but must obtain it by eating (consuming) other organisms.

convection Transfer of heat through a liquid or gas by the movement of the liquid or gas.

Coriolis effect The apparent deflection of a body that is moving toward or away from the equator. It is caused by the rotation of the Earth beneath the moving body. The magnitude of the Coriolis effect varies with speed and latitude; it is zero at the equator and at a maximum at the poles. Bodies traveling away from the equator appear to move to the east, those moving toward the equator to the west. The effect was first explained by French physicist Gaspard de Coriolis in 1835.

cork Protective tissue that covers the surface of the trunk and branches of woody plants. It consists of dead cells coated with a waxy substance, suberin, that makes them waterproof.

deciduous Seasonally shed, like the leaves of certain trees and the antlers of deer. The word is sometimes applied to structures, such as the scales of some fish, that are shed readily (although not seasonally).

dew point temperature The temperature at which water vapor condenses and liquid water evaporates. Dew point temperature varies according to the amount of water vapor present in the air (the humidity).

ecology The study of the relationships among living organisms in a defined area and between the organisms and the nonliving features of their surroundings.

ecosystem A community of living organisms and their nonliving environment within a defined area. This may be of any size. A forest may be studied as an ecosystem and so may a drop of water.

eutrophic Highly enriched in nutrients.

evergreen Although all leaves die and are shed, those of an evergreen plant are not all shed at the same time, so the plant retains leaves throughout the year. Most conifers are evergreen, as are some broad-leaved trees, such as holly.

fen An area of land that is wet for much of the time and is made up largely of peaty soil that is alkaline or neutral (not acid).

front A boundary between two masses of air that are at different temperatures.

fungus A soft-bodied organism that obtains nutrients by absorbing them from its surroundings. Fungi are neither plants nor animals but constitute a kingdom of their own, the Fungi.

ground water Water below ground that fills all the spaces between soil particles, saturating the soil.

gymnosperm A plant in which the ovule, bearing seeds, is not enclosed in an ovary but is carried naked on the surface of a modified leaf. In most gymnosperms the modified leaves form the scales of cones.

heartwood The dead wood at the center of a tree trunk.

herbivore An animal that feeds exclusively on plants.

insectivore An animal that feeds mainly or exclusively on insects.

invertebrate An animal that does not have a backbone.

jet stream A fast-moving stream of air at high altitude, produced by the sharp difference in temperature between the masses of air on either side, and flowing from east to west. There are two principal jet streams in each hemisphere. The subtropical jet stream occurs at the front between tropical and temperate air, the polar jet stream at the front between temperate and polar air.

lichen A plantlike organism consisting of a fungus and either an alga or a cyanobacterium (a bacterium that carries out photosynthesis) living in close association. The visible part of a lichen may be crustlike, scaly, leafy, or shrubby.

lignin A tough, chemically inert compound found in many of the cell walls of plants. It toughens the cell walls and in woody plants survives the death of the cells.

lignotuber A woody outgrowth at the base of the trunk that is found in many perennial plants growing in a Mediterranean climate. Lignotubers contain dormant buds that sprout if the main stem is severely damaged.

litter Plant and animal remains that lie on the ground. Litter includes dead leaves, twigs, fallen fruits, and animal droppings.

lung The organ of respiration in air-breathing vertebrates. In land-dwelling mollusks (snails and slugs), the part of the body involved in respiration.

montane Of mountainous regions.

muskeg An area of bog that is found in the taiga. It usually has bog moss (*Sphagnum* species) and cotton sedge (*Eriophorum* species) and sometimes a few stunted trees.

omnivore An animal that eats food derived from both plants and animals.

parasite An organism that lives on the surface, or inside the body, of another organism. The parasite is usually smaller than its host and gets food, shelter, or some other necessity from it. The effects of the parasite on its host may range from none at all to severe illness or death.

petiole The stalk connecting a leaf to its stem.

phellogen *See* cambium.

phloem Tissue made up of channels through which nutrient substances arc transpoited in solution to all parts of a plant.

photosynthesis The series of chemical reactions by which green plants manufacture sugars, getting hydrogen from water and carbon from carbon dioxide, the energy driving the reactions being provided by light that is absorbed by chlorophyll.

phytoplankton *See* plankton.

plankton The small organisms that live near the surface of water and drift with movements of the water. They include single-celled plants (phytoplankton) and small animals (zooplankton), some of which are the larvae of fish and crustaceans.

predator An organism that obtains food by consuming another organism. Most predators are animals that chase, overpower, and kill their prey, but insectivorous plants are also predators.

producer An organism, such as a green plant, that assembles large, complex substances from simple ingredients. These may then be eaten by consumers. On land the main producers are green plants; in water the main producers are phytoplankton (*see* plankton).

respiration 1 The oxidation of carbon to carbon dioxide in cells with the release of energy. **2** The action of breathing.

ring-barking Cutting through the bark of a tree all the way around the trunk in such a way as to sever all of the phloem vessels. This kills the tree by preventing the transport of sugars from the leaves to the roots.

sapwood The active xylem tissue that lies outside the heartwood in the trunk or branch of a woody plant.

sclerophyllous Having tough, thick, leathery, usually small, evergreen leaves as an adaptation to a climate with a hot, dry season.

spore A microscopically small structure from which, under favorable conditions, a new organism will develop. A spore contains genetic material but no embryo, and so is quite different from a seed.

succession A series of plant communities that follow one another during the establishment of a stable vegetation pattern (or "climax") in a particular area.

taiga The Russian name for the belt of coniferous forest that stretches across northern Eurasia. The name is often applied also to the similar North American forest (otherwise called the "boreal" forest). Some ecologists restrict the term "taiga" to the belt of open, parklike forest along the northern edge of the boreal forest.

transpiration The loss of water vapor through pores, called stomata in the leaves or lenticels in the stems, of green plants.

tropics Those parts of the world that lie between latitudes 23°30'N and 23°30'S. These latitudes mark the boundaries of the region within which the Sun is directly overhead at noon on at least one day each year. The Tropic of Cancer is to the north of the equator and the Tropic of Capricorn to the south.

vertebrate An animal that has a backbone. Vertebrates also have a bony skull containing the brain and a skeleton made from bone or cartilage. Fish, amphibians, reptiles, birds, and mammals are vertebrates.

water table The uppermost margin of the ground water, below which the soil is saturated and above which it is not, although it is still wet.

xanthophyll Any member of a group of compounds that are oxygenated derivatives of carotenes and form part of the larger group known as carotenoids.

xylem Tissue consisting of cells that form channels through which water entering through the roots is transported to all parts of a plant.

zooplankton *See* plankton.

Further Reading

Basics of Environmental Science by Michael Allaby. Routledge.

Biology by Neil A. Campbell. The Benjamin/Cummings Publishing Co. Inc.

The Encyclopedia of Birds edited by Christopher M. Perrins and Alex L.A. Middleton. Facts on File.

The Encyclopedia of Insects edited by Christopher O'Toole. Facts on File.

The Encyclopedia of Mammals edited by David Macdonald. Facts on File.

The Encyclopedia of Reptiles and Amphibians edited by Tim Halliday and Kraig Adler. Facts on File.

Flowering Plants of the World edited by V.H. Heywood. Oxford University Press, New York.

Green Planet edited by David M. Moore. Cambridge University Press.

The Hunters by Philip Whitfield. Simon and Schuster.

Hutchinson Encyclopedia of the Earth edited by Peter J. Smith. Hutchinson.

The Lie of the Land edited by K.J. Gregory. Oxford University Press, New York.

Longman Illustrated Animal Encyclopedia edited by Philip Whitfield. Guild Publishing.

The Oxford Encyclopedia of Trees of the World edited by Bayard Hora. Oxford University Press, New York.

Planet Earth: Cosmology, Geology, and the Evolution of Life and Environment by Cesare Emiliani. Cambridge University Press.

Snakes of the World by Chris Mattison. Blandford Press Ltd.

The Science of Ecology by Richard Brewer. Saunders College Publishing, Harcourt Brace College Publishers.

Ecosystems: Temperate Forests by Michael Allaby. Facts on File.

The Natural History of the USSR by Algirdas Knystautas. Century Hutchinson.

Natural Woodland: Ecology and Conservation in Northern Temperate Regions, by George F. Peterken. Cambridge University Press.

Photographic Acknowledgments

7 Vadim Gippenreiter; **8** Powerstock/Zefa Photo Library; **9** N.A. Callow/Natural History Photographic Agency; **15** Thonig/Powerstock/Zefa Photo Library; **16** Victor Englebert; **21** Fred Bruemmer; **23** Len Rue Jr.; **26** Oxford Scientific Films; **27** Frank Huber/Oxford Scientific Films; **32** Jacana; **42–43** David Woodfall/Natural History Photographic Agency; **45** J.P. Ferrero/Ardea London; **46** Carol Jopp/Robert Harding Picture Library; **51** Hans Reinhard/Bruce Coleman Limited; **52–53** Jacana; **Cover pictures:** *top*: Fritz Prenzel/Bruce Coleman Limited; *bottom*: David Hughes/Bruce Coleman Limited; *globe motif*: Terra Forma™ Copyright© 1995–1997 Andromeda Interactive Ltd.

While every effort has been made to trace the copyright holders of illustrations reproduced in this book, the publishers will be pleased to rectify any omissions or inaccuracies.

Set Index

Page numbers in *italics*
refer to illustrations; volume
numbers are in **bold**.